WE, THE PEOPLE OF GOD...

a *study of*
Constitutional Government
for the Church

edited by JAMES A. CORIDEN

Library of Congress Catalog Card Number: 68-23796
Copyright © Canon Law Society of America and Our Sunday Visitor Inc.
Published by Canon Law Society of America and Our Sunday Visitor Inc.
Printed in the United States of America by
OUR SUNDAY VISITOR, INC.
Huntington, Indiana 46750
826

TABLE OF CONTENTS

INTRODUCTION

+ Alexander Carter,

Bishop of Sault Ste. Marie

I have been asked to write an introduction to the book entitled "We, the People of God." I do so with pleasure. The book contains the Position Paper and various other Papers prepared by participants or resulting from proceedings of the Symposium entitled "A Constitution for the Church." Sponsored by the Canon Law Society of America and Fordham University, the Symposium brought together an interesting and varied group of scriptural scholars, theologians, philosophers, historians, sociologists, experts in Canon and Civil Law. Fitting perhaps into none of these categories were Bishop Primeau and myself!

A glance at the names of those who participated in the discussions reveals that the reader must not look for a unilateral approach to the fundamental question under consideration. Nor should he expect a simplistic answer to the complex problems involved in any study. In justice to those who participated I must add that the reader should remember that discussions were limited to a week-end. Many fundamental questions therefore remain untouched. These Papers are expressions of opinions. The Position Paper is a tentative document which aims at supplying material for further study and discussion. It is not meant to be nor is it by any means a definitive solution to the problems underlying a constitutional form of government for the Church.

These observations do not belittle the value of the work. On the contrary. The very difference of opinion among the participants proves the need for just such a stimulating and challenging approach to the questions which bedevil the Church in the modern world. While we did not agree on everything we all did agree on some things. Perhaps the most interesting and intriguing fact is that we early renounced our original project. We had come together to propose the elements for "a Constitution for the Church." We ended by doubting whether such a Constitution could or should ever be fully formulated or reduced to written form! It was judged wiser and preferable to develop some principles which would influence the present and future structures of the Church. Hence the name "Towards Constitutional Development Within The Church."

It is not my intention to enter a plea for the opinions expressed in this book of proceedings. Neither do I intend to give my own opinions. I simply ask that each one read it with an open mind free to accept or reject, debate or challenge its content. It is not meant to close but to open discussion. Some may discern a lack of cohesiveness and apparent contradictions. But this I maintain. The basic values which are sought are the values which the Church must incorporate if she is to fulfill her mission in the modern world. The documents of Vatican II will do no good reposing quietly on the book shelves of the clergy, in the libraries of institutions, or even in paperback form in the homes of some of our good lay people. Vatican II was more than the sum of its documents. It was a living experience of the Church, a stirring of the Spirit of the God in the People of God—in modern terms "a happening." We have been summoned by the Spirit of God as members of His Church to be in reality a sacrament of the world. But what world if not this world in which we live? This modern world where a breathless breakthrough of knowledge and know-how has revolutionized every facet of human life.

Could the Church as a living and throbbing reality escape this explosion? Would it even be desirable that she do so. Let those who bewail the ferment that has followed the Council tell us if it is preferable that the Church be a sleeping beauty in the midst of such intense life and activity. She would cease to be the Church; she would betray her mission; she would repudiate Christ with "whose incarnational mission in the world and in history" she is identified.

The contributors to these pages have done an excellent job in putting before us some fundamental questions. The institutional Church, as some insist upon calling it, is in a state of siege. Part of the criticism is unjust, part of it is valid and founded. We are indebted today to all who help us to find a solution to anguishing problems which the Church faces. The stress here upon the freedom of the individual, the dignity of the human person, the pastoral mission of the Church fulfilled in the context of man's growing consciousness of community—all this is of the utmost importance. It supplies the context in which the structures of the Church may evolve so as not to restrict and hamper and suffocate, but to release and free the human spirit as mankind seeks to fulfill its manifest destiny while the Church recalls the lordship of Christ and proclaims the freedom of the children of God.

It is good that the Society of Canon Law should indicate that the laws of the Church are to assure and guarantee this freedom. Law in the Church cannot be understood save as a pastoral reality. Structures are necessary—they are necessary to guarantee the saving action of Christ in His Church. Without them the community quickly becomes a mob. But they are a positive not a negative element. Hence the insistence here on the principle of subsidiarity which underlies many of the conclusions is of prime and capital importance. Of equal import is the wish to see the whole community involved in the law-making process. The concrete suggestions incorporated in the various papers may or may not be acceptable to the reader. Obviously they were not acceptable to all the participants in the Symposium. There is a difficult area of theological interpretation of the role of the hierarchy, the rights and duties of Bishops and how they are to be reconciled with the participation of the community. The opinions voiced here are no more than that and are meant to stimulate and begin not terminate discussion.

However the principles we have just mentioned can hardly be repudiated by anyone who pretends to be in the stream of Catholic thinking of our time. To repudiate them is to repudiate the encyclicals *Mater et Magistra* and *Pacem in Terris* of Pope John and *Populorum Progressio* of Pope Paul. It is to repudiate the whole tenor of Vatican II, especially the Pastoral Constitution on the Church in the Modern World. If any would reject them let them do so but not in the name of orthodoxy or on the pretence that they are contrary to Catholic teaching and "offensive to pious ears!"

It was the hope of the group that they could be of help in presenting the principles which must govern participation by all segments of the community in the deliberative and decision-making processes. Once again there are areas of disagreement. A long tradition will not change overnight. A wide variety of opinions exist on what is desirable and what is feasible within the Church. These were for the most part men of experience not starry-eyed dreamers or woolly-headed theorizers. They are aware of the difficulties involved. They suggest solutions at the various levels of the Church. Simply to reject these attempts at solution is no answer. Let those who have better ones to offer step forward and do so. Few should deny that some solutions are necessary.

Nor is it an answer to say that there are grave difficulties involved. The principle of collegiality brought the same difficulties to the discussions in Vatican II. How in practice were we to conciliate the personal authority of the Pope with the universal responsibility of the Bishops? This question was left unsettled. An experience was to be lived, an experience which under the guidance of the Holy Spirit would reveal the answer. The first hesitant or preparatory step has been taken in the Synod of Bishops. The same is true of the Bishop in his diocese, with his clergy, with his people. The parish priest in his parish or the priest who is to animate other communities as the needs arise must also live and learn. Where there is love and unity there will be no difficulty. Where there is trust and mutual respect things will go well. But good will alone is not enough. A plan must be initiated. The elements of a plan are suggested here. Let the debate begin but for heaven's sake let us have the debate.

Without endorsing every statement I believe that the reader will find much of interest in the principles suggested for the judicial and administrative process of the Church. Some may even find that there is an overstress on this institutional aspect of the Church. Unfortunately law is necessary. Men are men and misunderstandings arise. The strength of the present approach is the positive interpretation of law. It is treated as an instrument to foster and protect not as a coercive or prohibitory influence. The insistence upon due process is particularly welcome to one who cherishes freedom. If much of what is said about administration on the diocesan level applies only to large and well organized dioceses, the principles involved have a certain validity for all.

I find it hard to quarrel with the conviction that the administration of justice or administrative procedures in general should be as open as possible. Surely we are learning the hard way that the Church cannot live and function in a conspiracy of silence. This is true of every facet of its life.

If the Lay Apostolate Congress received better and more intelligent coverage than the Synod of Bishops in Rome it was because it was open and hospitable to the representatives of the mass media. We cannot ignore the culture in which we live and are immersed. Even if we don't like it, it won't go away! I hope that the present work will stimulate real and live discussion in this whole area and lead to some conclusions. It is a pressing problem and the reasons for solving it are compelling.

In the Position Paper we read (VII, [4]) "Any formulation of law must reflect an awareness and assimilation of the cumulative knowledge and experience, not only of the Church, but of all mankind, especially as available in modern disciplines, i.e., psychology, sociology, history, etc. Organic assimilation of these resources will always reflect the distinctive character of the Christian community." I could not agree more. This was one experience of the Symposium. Experts from various disciplines exercise a salutary and disciplinary influence upon one another. The day of the expert in all things—if it ever existed—is over. The Church, whether universal or local, needs all its sons and daughters. It needs their knowledge, their charisms, their active contribution. We must work together. The magisterium, without denying or abdicating its role and its responsibilities, must not stand aside in hurt silence. It must call in trust and confidence to all the people of God. We bishops must show our faith and confidence in the good sense and wisdom of our people. The *sensus fidelium* functions in the Church. In the long run it will better contain the loud mouth and self seeker than will an arbitrary or authoritative use of power. The time for the oratorical calls upon the "good lay people" to take their rightful place in the Church is over. We must now get down to the more demanding task of ways and means. We must forge the instruments and find the tools. Otherwise they can accuse us of insincerity. It is not the aggressive members we must fear, even if they are occasionally tiresome. Let us rather fear the indifferent. When our people don't care any more it will be too late.

The priest must inspire and give a new spiritual dimension to those to whom he ministers and from whom he learns. Old fears and suspicions must be put aside and the welcome mat extended to all who bring their knowledge and knowhow to the Church. The layman, emerging or not, must take the chip off his shoulder, not confuse his personal opinions with those of the People of God, tone down the stridency of his voice and be humble enough to believe that the bishop or the pastor really wants to share with him the mission of the Church. Or, at the other end of the spectrum, the layman must awaken from his long sleep and realize that he has responsibility, that he too has a prophetic and priestly role to play, and get with it. If this little book provokes some agreement, some disagreement, some discussion, some searching, "We, the People of God" will be the beneficiaries.

✠ALEXANDER CARTER
Bishop of Sault Ste. Marie

EDITOR'S PREFACE

James A. Coriden

This book is the result of a Symposium entitled "A Constitution for the Church." The Symposium was held at the Statler-Hilton Hotel in New York City on October 7-9, 1967. It was sponsored by the Canon Law Society of America and Fordham University, and it was made possible by a grant from Our Sunday Visitor, Inc.

It is important to understand the background to this project. The mandate to renew and update the Church's law was given by Pope John XXIII on January 29, 1959, the same occasion on which he called for the Ecumenical Council. On March 28, 1962, shortly before his death, Pope John named a Pontifical Commission for the Revision of the Code of Canon Law. He instructed this group to receive recommendations from the conciliar commissions, but he said that their work of collation and formulation would not begin in earnest until after the conclusion of the Council. Pope Paul VI added members of the Commission on November 7, 1963, and November 13, 1965, and he appointed more than one hundred consultants to the Commission. In his remarks to the Commission on November 20, 1965, Pope Paul suggested the possibility of "a fundamental and common Code which contains the constitutive law of the Church."

This "fundamental law of the Church" has been widely discussed since that time, and some attempts at formulation have been made.

Although no draft of a *ius constitutivum ecclesiae* was found acceptable for presentation to the Synod of Bishops which convened on September 29, 1967, the notion of such a general, fundamental law was the subject of much of the bishops' discussions. The summary remarks of Archbishop Pericle Felici, newly appointed chairman of the Commission for Revision, at the end of the Synod's deliberations on Canon Law indicated a favorable attitude toward the idea, and it is certain that further efforts will be made to design and propose a fundamental law for the universal Church.

The Canon Law Society of America has as its stated purpose "to participate in the constant renewal of Canon Law by engaging in, encouraging, and aiding canonical research and studies, and by proposing such revisions of the law as the changing circumstances of time or place may suggest." One attempt to fulfill that purpose was a Seminar sponsored by the Society in Pittsburgh, October 8-10, 1966. The Seminar was on "The Role of Law in the Church" and it included a wide representation of scholars from various disciplines and religious traditions. The proceedings of the Seminar, edited by James E. Biechler, were published by Helicon in 1967 in a book entitled *Law for Liberty*. The conclusions of that study session called for many of the values and structures in the future law of the Church which we identify with western constitutionalism. Since it has long been a suspicion (not to say pre-judgment) of many members of the Canon Law Society that the Church could learn from the Anglo-American common law tradition, the proposal for a "constitutional" study was eagerly forwarded and well received. It is to the credit of the Board of Governors of the Society, under the leadership of Father Alan McCoy, O.F.M., that they wholeheartedly authorized the Symposium project at their meeting in February, 1967.

Father Christopher Mooney, S.J., chairman of the Department of Theology of Fordham University, when approached about the possibilities of cooperation in the Symposium, responded with his characteristic openness and encouragement. Since that time, Fordham's support and collaboration has been complete, cordial, and more than competent.

Bishop Leo A. Pursley of Fort Wayne-South Bend, President of Our Sunday Visitor, Inc., received the request for financial assistance with understanding, and, the Board of Directors, acting with vision and concern for the renewal of the Church, approved the proposal. A lasting debt of recognition and gratitude is owed to them.

Father Peter Shannon of Chicago, the genial and efficient

"business agent" for the Symposium, gave inspiration and imaginative assistance at crucial moments in the planning and execution of the project.

Many, many others, lay persons, and religious, priests and bishops, gave generously of their wisdom and counsel during the preparatory stages of the Symposium. Some were eventually participants, but many others were not. Without their encouragement the event would not have occurred; without their sage advice it would have been superficial.

In addition to numerous interviews and personal conversations in various parts of the country, four local conferences were held in preparation for the Symposium. These took place in Chicago (on September 23), at the Law School of the University of California, Berkeley (Sept. 24), at the Center for the Study of Democratic Institutions, Santa Barbara (Sept. 25), and at Emmanuel College, Boston (Sept. 30). To those who hosted and participated in these valuable meetings, a special word of gratitude is due. Their reflections and observations raised many pertinent issues. They stimulated and refined the thinking of the participants in the Symposium.

Regarding the contents of the book, a word of explanation is in order. The Position Paper, "Toward Constitutional Development Within the Church," is the heart of the publication. It was originated, developed, and finished within the few hours of the Symposium, and is the product of the intense efforts of all the participants. The brief report of the Symposium discussions is inserted as an attempt to capture some of the "sparks of dialogue." It is a minimal indication of the exchange, fascinating and disparate, which took place. It provides an example of the rationale behind such interdisciplinary seminars: the dialogic nature of truth. Several persons looking at a problem from different perspectives can tell one another much more about it than any one viewpoint can reveal.

Father Peter Huizing's brief "Notes" were written shortly after the Symposium in response to a request to give his reactions to the project.

The chapters by Heston, Greeley, Warwick, Tierney, Hess, Fontinell, and Bridston were papers written prior to the Symposium and distributed in advance to the participants. The authors were asked for "statements of position" or informal presentations, rather than detailed research pieces. They were given the opportunity to revise their contributions after the Symposium, and some made minor changes or additions.

Mr. Zizola's article was published by Information Documentation on the Conciliar Church (IDO-C) just before the dates of the Symposium. It is included here, with the kind permission of IDO-C, to supplement Father Heston's description of the present government of the Church, and to describe the attempt at reform which is presently being made at the highest level.

Father Murray's paper originally appeared in *America* magazine (December 3, 1966). On May 9, 1967, he agreed to prepare a paper for the Symposium (which he also planned to attend) applying some of the principles in his article to the organizational reform of the Church. Father Murray's health declined during the summer, and he died suddenly on August 16. His paper is included here, with the gracious assent of the editors of *America*, because of its precise relevance to the issues under consideration, and because it was widely quoted during the Symposium and had a marked influence on the thought of the participants.

Those who took part in the dynamic exchange of the Symposium were in complete agreement on one important point: the critical need for the maximum participation of the whole community in the process of renewing the Church's legal structure. The Position Paper and the other chapters contained in this book are presented in an effort to stimulate discussion of these issues as widely as possible. May God's Holy Spirit inspire and direct these deliberations to the upbuilding and invigoration of the Body of Christ. May the Church stand before the world as a "demonstration community" wherein each man's freedom, dignity, and responsibility are honestly honored and manifestly protected.

JAMES A. CORIDEN

I.
REPORT FROM
THE SYMPOSIUM

PARTICIPANTS:

Rt. Rev. Myles M. Bourke, Theology Department, Fordham University

Rev. Paul M. Boyle, C.P., Executive Coordinator, Canon Law Society, St. Meinrad Seminary

Dr. Keith R. Bridston, Pacific Lutheran Theological Seminary, Berkeley

Most Rev. Alexander Carter, Bishop of Sault Ste. Marie

Rev. James A. Coriden, Chancery, Diocese of Gary

Rev. James C. Finlay, S.J., Political Science Department, Fordham University

Mr. Eugene Fontinell, Philosophy Department, Queen's College, New York

Mr. William Gorman, Center for Study of Democratic Institutions, Santa Barbara

Rev. Andrew M. Greeley, National Opinion Research Center, University of Chicago

Mr. Hamilton Hess, Theology Department, University of San Francisco

Rev. Peter Huizing, S.J., University of Nijmegen, Holland

Rt. Rev. Stephen J. Kelleher, Tribunal, Archdiocese of New York

Rev. L. Mason Knox, Grace Church, Yantic, Connecticut

Rev. Bernard J. F. Lonergan, S.J., Regis College, Ontario

Rev. Richard P. McBrien, Pope John XXIII Seminary, Weston, Mass.

Rev. Alan McCoy, O.F.M., President, Canon Law Society, Oakland, California

Rev. John M. McGrath, Canon Law School, Catholic University of America

Mr. Mark R. MacGuigan, Law School, University of Windsor

Rev. Frederick R. McManus, Canon Law School, Catholic University of America

Rev. Adam J. Maida, Chancery, Diocese of Pittsburgh

Mr. John H. Mansfield, Law School, Harvard University

Rev. Christopher F. Mooney, S.J., Theology Department, Fordham University

Rev. Daniel J. O'Hanlon, S.J., Alma College, Los Gatos, California

Rev. Ladislas Orsy, S.J., Theology Department, Fordham University

Most Rev. Ernest J. Primeau, Bishop of Manchester

Rt. Rev. John S. Quinn, St. Andrew's Church, Chicago

Miss Miriam Theresa Rooney, Law School, Seton Hall University

Rev. Peter M. Shannon, Tribunal, Archdiocese of Chicago

Rev. Thomas P. Swift, S.J., Theology Department, St. Louis University

Mr. Brian Tierney, History Department, Cornell University

Mr. Donald Warwick, Social Relations Department, Havard University

Rev. Charles Whalen, S.J., Law School, Fordham University

Towards Constitutional

Development within the Church

POSITION PAPER

I / Introduction The revision of the Code of Canon Law, currently in process, will play an important part, for good or evil, in the renewal of the Church. Conscious of the need for serious study, the Canon Law Society of America sponsored an interdisciplinary seminar in October, 1966, on the Role of Law in the Church. The recommendations from this study session pointed toward many of the values and structures found in a constitutional form of government.

With this as the background, the Canon Law Society in conjunction with Fordham University, under a grant from Our Sunday Visitor, Inc., sponsored a symposium (Oct. 7-9, 1967) in New York to explore the possibilities of a constitutional form of government for the Church. Scripture scholars, theologians, philosophers, historians, sociologists, and experts in canon and civil law presented papers and exchanged reactions to them. Although profoundly aware of the limitations imposed by the shortness of the time available for their deliberations, the participants have nonetheless attempted a tentative position paper entitled "Towards Constitutional Development Within the Church."

5

Participants in the symposium wish to emphasize that there was much division of opinion and even radical disagreement in their two-and-one-half days of deliberation. Since, however, the Church's canon law is already in the process of revision, the symposium participants have unanimously agreed to present these views to the Vatican Commission for the Revision of the Code of Canon Law and also to the community at large, in order to initiate reflection and to promote discussion and comment.

II / General Principles to Guide Development

By way of preface, it should be noted that one of the most fundamental juridical facts is the existence of various Rites within the Catholic Church. It is essential to the process of developing constitutionalism that these Rites continue their proper life, with their own hierarchy, liturgy and canonical tradition. We hope to learn from their insights and that they will be responsive to ours.

Constitutional renewal, moreover, must look forward to future union with other Christian Churches (Eastern and Western) on a similar basis, i.e., with the maintenance, so far as possible, of their distinctive canonical and liturgical traditions and of their own hierarchy.

We do not look, therefore, for a fully formulated constitution for the Church either now or in the near future. Indeed, we leave open the question whether such a constitution could or should ever be fully formulated or reduced to written form.

In so far, however, as the self-consciousness of the Christian way of life continues to express itself in every age and this expression tends to become normative for the Church, we think some principles can and should be formulated to guide the constitutional development of the Church.

THEOLOGICAL PRINCIPLES

The Second Vatican Council adopted a method of correlation in its Pastoral Constitution on the Church in the Modern World, where it constructed its self-understanding of the Church's mission in terms of a response to the situation as it really is. The Council referred to these realities as "signs of the times."

6

In proposing a theological context within which constitutional principles may be devised for the Church, one can readily and usefully pursue this same theological method. What, indeed, are the relevant "signs of the times?" The first is man's growing consciousness of his dignity as a person, which requires that he act on his responsibility and therefore in freedom. The second is man's growing consciousness of community, of that being with others and for others which is revealed, for instance, in the phenomenon of "socialization" in the sense of *Mater et Magistra* and is fundamental in *Populorum Progressio.*

In point of fact, the Church's emerging reflective awareness of her nature and mission (ecclesiology) corresponds organically with these distinctive "signs of the times." The Church is beginning to understand herself more clearly as a genuinely human community whose essential mark of identity is that she explicitly and publicly acknowledges the Lordship of Jesus Christ, affirming that what is happening, has happened and will happen in history makes sense because of the life and ministry, death and resurrection of Jesus of Nazareth. (In traditional terms, this is the Church's *kerygmatic* function.) The Church is a community which understands her mission as one with Christ's and which identifies herself with his ongoing, incarnational mission in the world and in history.

Accordingly, the Church is a community which, in addition to its kerygmatic function, exists to create and to respond to genuine human community. (This is the Church's task of *diakonia,* of service in and for the larger community of mankind.) And, finally, the Church must offer itself as a kind of model, or sign of a genuine human community, and as such the Christian community should inspire confidence in the ultimate direction and course of human history. (This is the Church's function of *koinonia,* of fellowship.)

Any constitutional principles for the Church must be subordinated to this three-fold missionary responsibility which the whole Christian community shares through the power of the indwelling Spirit. These principles must facilitate, expedite, and actively encourage and promote the mission of the Church. Any legal or procedural realities which obstruct this mission *in any way* are to be revised accordingly or simply revoked. Nothing in the Church is superior to her mission. Indeed, the mission itself is more important than the Church (which is to say, in traditional theological language, that the Church is always subordinate to the Kingdom of God).

7

THEOLOGY AND PRINCIPLES OF CONSTITUTIONALISM

Given this particular ecclesiological context, it would seem that certain recognized principles of constitutionalism might be employed in the Church, at least analogically.

Firstly, since authority is exercised within and for the entire community and ultimately derived from the Word of God, the power of all those individuals and groups possessing authority within the Church is limited, and ways to make the limitations effective must be found. The institutions which, in our opinion, are most relevant as limitations of power are the following: (1) a division of power between central and regional governing bodies; (2) the separation of legislative, executive, and judicial power; and (3) guarantees of individual rights, including due process of law.

Secondly, because all authority in the Church, as exercised by such individuals or groups, is for the service of the Church in the fulfillment of her three-fold mission, then there must be some means whereby those in authority are to be held accountable and responsible to those whom they are supposed to serve. The institutions which are most relevant here are the following: (1) the electoral process; (2) freedom of information, whereby the exercise of official power is a matter of public record; and (3) freedom of discussion and debate regarding the policy and performance of office holders as well as the ultimate assumptions of the community itself.

Thirdly, any constitutional principles devised must be permanently open to experimentation and must contain within themselves the means and program of perennial self-correction, because of the recognition that law is merely a means to the achievement of social ends and, consequently, demands revision as social conditions change. This juridical principle is fulfilled in secular societies by various means, the most important of which are these: (1) regular meetings of legislative bodies; (2) re-interpretation of law by tribunals; and (3) permanent commissions charged with the responsibility of proposing legal reforms.

III / General Principles for Legislative Process

We are living a new experience. We know that there must be universal participation in the deliberative process by which laws are formed, but we cannot know or prescribe *a priori* the forms through which such participation should evolve in the institutions and experiences of the Church.

The motivating principle for the development of deliberative structures at every level in the Church is the co-responsibility of all its members to continue the mission of Christ in the world. In establishing these structures, the Church will bring to bear the wisdom, experience and insight of all its members for the more effective achievement of its mission.

Bishops participate in such legislative bodies of the Church in virtue of their episcopal office. All others will participate because of the presence of the Spirit in the whole Christian community and as a matter of canonical equity. Participation by all is necessary in order for all to fulfill their obligations as members of the Church and to join with the Pope, the bishops and the pastors in their service of mankind. Such participation conforms to modern theological formulations as well as to ancient canonical practice.

In the development of legislative bodies the aim should be the maximum feasible participation by all segments of the community in the deliberative and decision-making processes. At all levels at least these fundamental conditions should be fulfilled:

(1) The body should meet regularly according to its own rules.

(2) The body should choose its own officers and determine its own rules of procedure and agenda.

(3) The deliberations of the body should be open and should be publicized.

(4) The body should have its own secretariat, with full access to relevant information and with the assistance of experts.

It is evident that the exercise of what is understood as a canonical legislative power will be of greater or less concern in various deliberative assemblies. In the present state of canonical institutes, the diocesan bishop would thus exercise his legislative power in the diocesan council or assembly, and members of an episcopal conference would exercise their legislative power in a national council or assembly. The desirable direction of constitutional evolution in the Church is for these bodies to broaden the legislative process by their own activities and to provide opportunities for greater and greater participation by all segments of the community.

PARISH COUNCIL

When we speak of "parishes" or other local communities of Christians, we are fully aware that while traditional, territorial parishes are likely to continue, other forms of community are being studied and are developing.

There should be a parish council or assembly, selected by the community and representing all segments of the community.

The council should be the policy-making body for the community. Its decisions should be reached on the basis of a consensus of the pastor and the representatives of the community, with due regard for the rights and opinions of the associate pastors, the religious serving the community, and the people.

DIOCESAN COUNCIL

In every diocese a policy-making council or legislative assembly should be established in which the clergy, religious and laity can all fully participate. All groups within the diocese should be represented in the council, whether these groups are gathered together in parishes, other local communities, or still other organizations which will and should be developed to speak for the various groups.

The deliberation of the council should conform to the four fundamental norms set forth above. Decisions should be reached on the basis of a consensus of the bishop and the representatives of the community.

NATIONAL COUNCIL

There should be a national council or legislative assembly representing all the orders of the Church (laity, religious, clergy and bishops) to articulate the needs and, in appropriate spheres, establish policy for the Church within the nation. This council would complement the work of the present episcopal conference.

The principle of subsidiarity may also require the existence in some nations of regional conferences to consider specifically regional problems.

UNIVERSAL SYNOD

The present Synod of Bishops should function in virtue of the episcopal collegiality of its members and not merely as a consultative body to the Pope. Legislation for the whole Church should be enacted according to the collegial principle.

Provision should next be made for representation of all orders of the Church in this synod.

All the fundamental conditions outlined above for a deliberative body should be observed by the synod.

ECUMENICAL COUNCIL

Similarly, when an ecumenical council is convened, all the fundamental conditions for a deliberative organ outlined above should be observed.

IV / General Principles for Judicial System

Law can positively facilitate the development of the People of God. Ecclesiastical courts should creatively interpret law and, in so doing, contribute to the life and mission of the Church. Law should not be viewed primarily as coercive or prohibitory, but rather as an instrument for fostering and protecting the creative freedom of the members of the Christian community.

The experience of many nations has demonstrated the wisdom of some functional separation of the executive, legislative and judicial power at the practical level of government. The Church could benefit greatly from adopting, in so for as possible, this type of government.

For the proper discharge of the judicial function in the Church, there seems to be a need today for two classes of tribunals:

(1) formal courts

(2) boards of "mediation and arbitration"

11

The decisions of formal courts are binding on the parties. The decisions of boards of mediation and arbitration are not binding on the parties; either party, if dissatisfied, may invoke a formal court. The authority of the decisions of boards of mediation and arbitration shall derive from the inherent fairness of these decisions, from the publicity given to them, and from the standing of the judges who have rendered them.

While the existence of these two types of courts appears to be necessary at present, we hope that in many instances the securing of rights will be assured by procedures other than judicial.

The integrity of the judicial system depends upon the independence of the judges. This independence should be fostered by all appropriate means.

FORMAL COURTS

Regional courts should be developed under the aegis of the episcopal conferences.

Parties should be fully apprised during the proceedings of the evidence upon which the decisions of formal courts will be based, and the parties should be given full opportunity to argue all the issues in dispute.

The procedure of formal courts should aim at simplicity and speed. Local and regional courts should give due consideration to the local and regional customs, culture, and ideas of procedural justice.

Courts should give the reasons for their decisions and should afford opportunity for the expression of judicial dissents.

The only criterion for personnel in the courts should be professional competence. No one should be disqualified on grounds of sex or lack of clerical status.

In so far as possible, formal courts should be staffed by full-time and professionally trained personnel.

Judges should be appointed for a term of years. In the interest of their independence, they should not be removable by executive order.

The binding interpretation of the laws of the Church should

be reserved to the courts; executive offices or commissions should not have the right to make such interpretations.

The procedure in marriage cases should be as simple, flexible and expeditious as possible because:

(1) the subject matter of the case is theological, i.e., the existence of a sacrament;

(2) the most intimate rights of the parties are concerned;

(3) the proceeding is not truly adversary;

(4) the relevant evidence can often be collected from the parties themselves;

(5) delay can cause irreparable injustice to the parties and to their children.

BOARDS OF MEDIATION AND ARBITRATION

There are many disputes which arise in the Church wherein the parties do not want to go formally to court. To solve these disputes in a spirit of fairness and charity, there should be a system of boards of arbitration and mediation. These boards should take on the following character:

(1) their procedure should be informal, prompt, and adapted to local ideas and customs;

(2) the aim and purpose of the boards is a common-sense, equitable solution to the disputes brought before them;

(3) clergy, religious and laymen should actively participate in the structure and operation of these boards. Every effort should be made to find judges acceptable to the parties to the dispute.

V / General Principles of Administration

It should be assumed as a guiding principle that individuals operating within the administration of the Church will enjoy the greatest amount of human dignity and will perform most effectively when:

(1) they are given the maximum amount of autonomy and

13

responsibility consistent with the overall goals of the administrative office;

(2) there is free communication between them and their superiors, when they are able to exercise influence over these superiors, and when the superiors provide the necessary support for the individual to carry out his work;

(3) decisions affecting the operation of the office filled by an individual are reached collectively by the office holder in collaboration with his superiors and co-laborers, rather than imposed from above through administrative edict.

Recruitment for administrative positions in the Church should ordinarily be based upon the qualifications of available candidates.

Persons working within the administrative structures of the Church should be allowed the freedom, responsibility and scope for initiative common to professionals of similar training in their own societies. Included in this concept of professional status is the possibility of orderly advancement on the basis of merit rather than seniority, the consideration of individual preferences and abilities in the assignment process, and opportunities for continued training to maintain an adequate level of professional competence.

All major divisions of Church administration (international, national, diocesan) should develop structured means of research, planning, and internal criticism to obtain an adequate understanding of progress as well as deficiencies in administration. Such possibilities as the following should be considered and adopted when feasible:

(1) An office devoted to research and planning for the long-range development of the Church at the central, national, diocesan or parish level;

(2) An office of financial management responsible for accounting and accountability to the Church at large;

(3) Permanent means of assessing public opinion in the Church, e.g., through such techniques as probability samples and interviews with members;

(4) A "public relations" department whose function would be to provide information to Church members and the public at large on policies, procedures and related matters in the Church.

COMPOSITION OF THE CENTRAL ADMINISTRATION

The Pope and Synod, in their service of the Universal Church, are assisted by a Curia, which serves in an advisory, executive and administrative capacity.

Since the Curia is a transnational organization with operations throughout the world, it would seem that proper staffing of the Curia would necessarily require the utilization of personnel from many nations.

Major officials of the Curia should be changed at stated intervals in order to make certain that they actually represent the current mind and needs of the Church.

To provide for the selection of suitable personnel for the Curia, it would seem advisable to establish an Appointment Board constituted of persons from various countries. The appointment of both major and minor officers should be made only after consultation with national conferences.

FUNCTION OF THE CENTRAL ADMINISTRATION

Decision-making falls into at least two distinct categories: basic policy determinations, and administrative directives to implement the basic determinations.

The making of general policy decisions at the level of the universal Church should be reserved to the Pope and Synod. The function of the Curia is to assist in the execution of these decisions. In the course of such execution, the Curia may issue administrative directives concerned with interdiocesan or supranational questions. The Curia should have no administrative authority in purely local matters.

ADMINISTRATION AT THE NATIONAL LEVEL

Powers which transcend the diocesan office of a bishop should be within the competence of the national conference of bishops, subject only to the provision that the national conferences of bishops should not act unilaterally on matters having an international impact.

Solution of cases involving acts of personal commitment

(such as marriage, religious vows and celibacy) should be decided on the local level according to norms and directives established by the Central Administration.

Methods should be devised to enable the local Church, acting through the national conference, to have an active and truly effective part in the selection of bishops.

It would seem advisable that dioceses should not be established or divided without recommendations to that effect by the national conference.

In addition to the national conference of bishops, other national organizations should be developed through which bishops, clergy, religious and laity can strive to make their contribution to the effective administration of the Church.

DIOCESAN ADMINISTRATION

Legislation for parishes must encourage various kinds of structural divisions to meet the needs of the community.

Religious and laity, as well as the clergy should be encouraged to participate in various planning and consultative bodies in the diocese. Let them also study to make their contribution through voluntary associations of their peers.

Structures, especially parochial, should be revised to insure genuine fraternal relationships among the clergy. One example would be greater reliance on team assignments.

The professional rights of all clergy should be specified in future statements of Church order. The law should further professional initiative and responsibility.

VI / Towards a Bill of Rights

In some of the documents of Vatican II, and in some of the encyclicals of John the XXIII and of Paul the VI, there has been explicit recognition of some of the fundamental rights of all human beings and, in particular, of all Christians.

Much more attention should be paid in the future, during the development of Church Law, to the legal protection of these human and Christian rights.

These rights may be classified broadly as substantive and procedural.

In the area of procedural rights particular attention should be paid to the presumption of innocence, and to the rights of confrontation, cross-examination, and assistance by competent and independent counsel.

In the area of substantive rights, particular attention should be paid to the right to the expression of honest opinion (especially in the academic forum), to the equality of women, lay or religious, in Church Law, and to the necessity for giving *de facto* as well as de iure protection to all persons regardless of race or national origin.

VII / Suggestions Concerning Methods of Development

(1) The process whereby good constitutional norms are embodied in the law of the Church demands extensive participation of all segments of the Church according to their capacity and competence. Indeed, all the general norms for full participation of all members of the Church (Section III), should also be normative for the ongoing process through which all the suggested forms of constitutionalism should be developed.

(2) Also the norms expressed for the judicial system of the Church (Section IV), are necessary for the process by which constitutionalism develops. Genuine protection of the creative freedom of all is a means for liberating those forces which move forward the process of constitutional development.

(3) Furthermore, all the suggestions of Section V, especially the remarks on Research and Planning, are applicable not only to the constitutional goal toward which this symposium is directed, but also the process by which this constitutional reality develops. Feedback, self-evaluation, open relationships, free flow of ideas, all these elements hasten the healthy constitutional development with which this symposium is concerned.

(4) Before any codification of new law or extension of old

17

institutions of law there should be a review of its necessity in terms of the changing life of the Church. Further, any formulation of law must reflect an awareness and assimilation of the cumulative knowledge and experience, not only of the Church, but of all mankind, especially as available in modern disciplines, i.e., psychology, sociology, history, etc. Organic assimilation of these resources will always reflect the distinctive character of the Christian community.

(5) In all these respects, the medium of mass communication offers multiple possibilities. For this reason the process of developing new formulations of law should not only be non-secretive, and in the public domain, but should in principle receive as wide publicity as possible during the period of formulation.

Points from the Discussions

Since there was no opportunity for thorough and orderly discussion of the symposium papers, no attempt has been made to record and represent the thread or sequence of our conversations. The following notes are simply a few of the moments or themes of the discussions, especially of some points not made in the prepared papers. The remarks are more often individual points of view than expressions of consensus.

The nature and source of authority is a common problem today. Perhaps the reality is that we *yield* authority to others gradually and in different ways, e.g., to parents, to teachers, to governors. This view of authority starts from "the bottom up," as in the common law tradition, from the individual to the one exercising some office in the community. However, even in the secular order, the theory of the nature and source of authority is far from clear.

Absolute authority at **any** level is bad, but in its exercise all authority is limited. Even though we might claim absolute authority for the pope in the Church, in fact his exercise of that authority is restricted in many ways, e.g., by the Curia, by public reaction, by the possibilities of the moment. The real question is how that power can best be limited for the good of the community, i.e., what forms its limited exercise should take. Paradoxically, the leader who consults has more power than the one who doesn't. The one who is forced to listen to the many sides of a problem and hear all the interested parties has more force behind his decisions than the one who makes the decisions in relative isolation and independently.

It is not always easy to "unload" responsibility in the Church today. Often a bishop who is eager to share some of his burdens has a hard time doing so simply because others are unwilling to assume them. The anomaly is that the newer structures for consensus-forming and consultation, e.g., priests' senates, pastoral commissions, etc., need constant "pushing" from the top, and do not spontaneously rise up to share authority.

*   *   *

Our ecumenical vision must be forward-looking. The object of our hope is not "reunion" or "return," but the ultimate convergence which lies in the future following the lines which the movement of the Spirit seems to be tracing for us.

There is a dangerous dualism or schizophrenia widespread in the churches today: an attempt to separate the organizational from the sacramental, the institutional from the charismatic. An increasing number of serious Christians have no time or use for the "organization" and claim that it has almost nothing to do with the gospel.

Every human community requires some kind of organization. Organization has to provide the framework and climate for the community to operate. Inefficient organization inhibits community; effective procedures can help it. Institutionalization can be a destructive, self-justifying force, but what the world needs now is the example of good institutions, those which assist and abet real community rather than stifle it. Healthy organization can be a "sign to the nations" as to how community can be aided, the person supported, and the love relationships between persons fostered.

A rupture between the world of reality and the world of values results in hallucination. The Church is in danger from this kind of conflict. The hallucination can take either of two forms: a utopianism, which maintains some kind of an ideal world and refuses to face problems; or reactionism, which rejects the values as unattainable in any way. Politics is the continuing struggle to maintain a balance or creative tension between the world of reality and the world of values. Politics is the opposite of hallucination.

*   *   *

This may well be the "last chance" for the Church. If it fails to reform radically, the Church may truly be "the grave of God." To debate minor adjustments in the laws of the Church at such a time is like tinkering with the inner mechanism of a ship while the whole vessel is sinking. This is a time of profound crisis. In our planning we must not underestimate the great gap between segments of the Christian community. To involve all segments and engage them in continuing conversation is a crucial and urgent necessity. The divergent elements and local communities must be "built into" the life of the Church.

*   *   *

We are in search of operative viable models for renewing our own structure, models which are not entrapping or rigidifying. For example, kinship models, like fatherhood, may not be as valuable today. The physical sciences, and, more proximately, the social sciences, should be able to provide us with models.

The British parliamentary system is one model that comes to mind. It has the advantage of working without a written constitution, and still achieving a balance of power. However, this analogue may be deficient when one considers that the monarchy has become largely ceremonial and symbolic. On the other hand, there have been times in the Church's history when the papacy was much more a symbol of unity than a center of power.

*   *   *

We are not uncomfortable in proposing western constitutional forms as possible models for the Church's government, not because we are narrowly western in outlook, but because these forms are increasingly prevalent and acknowledged as successful in the world of today. The spread and acceptance of these governmental forms indicates an historical trend.

A study of earlier history shows us that western constitutionalism is not foreign to our own Church tradition. We learn, rather, that what have become accepted as good modes of conduct in civil government have a long-standing affinity with the Church. Hence, we make these suggestions, not with embarrassment, but with pride.

The transition from the present monarchical style to more constitutional forms need not be a sharp break nor a disruptive shock. A gradual transmutation in the exercise of authority can take place beginning with the familiar instrument of delegation. For example, the pope could delegate some legislative power to a constitutional organ, like the Episcopal Synod, and custom would at once begin to influence its operation. By means of such enlightened, courageous acts of delegation, the Church could move toward a desirable decentralization, accountability, and balance of power.

*   *   *

A radically processive approach or developmental world-view leads one to the controlling assumption that every human institution must continually justify its own existence. If every institution is a creation of the community, developed to be of service in a time of need, then each one must be repeatedly examined and evaluated in the light of the needs of today. Institutions like the papacy and the episcopacy are given by God in the sense that He works in and through His community of believers. One cannot rule out the possibility *a priori* that an institution may have "had its day," may have ceased to serve as it was designed to historically. One cannot determine in advance the depth of change that is possible or necessary to meet the needs of today's community. The principles of evaluation, experimentation, and self-correction must be built into the structures of the present reform. We are not in transition between two fixed states, e.g., an "old" Church and a "new" one, we are simply "on the way." Our structures must be enabling, facilitating, not impeding.

*   *   *

There is a "normative given" that we cannot depart from. The content of the New Testament is a basic datum which is not changeable. We must decide to accept the canon of the New Testament as normative, and not simply as a monument of the past.

*   *   *

Law is a complex idea. It is wrong to look upon law as merely coercive or prohibitive. Law is a means to achieve ends; it is an enabling instrument. Perhaps what we need in the Church is not less law, but more! Different kinds of law, more sophisticated instruments, as in today's corporate law.

Sometimes we use the term "law" in a very wide sense to include many things which are not strictly juridical provisions. The Church might do better to employ less formal norms, regulations, standards, understandings, administrative procedures, etc., in preference to formal legal measures. They are often less onerous and they are easier to change.

*   *   *

The discussion on just what the Symposium group ought to do, what kind of recommendation it ought to make, ranged far and wide. The suggested possibilities include:

—formulate a written constitution for the Church, or at least the skeletal outline of one;

—issue a call for a constitutional convention, inclusive of all the segments of the "People of God," to debate and decide the elements of governmental reform;

—urge that a written constitution not be attempted, since it might be least desirable in this time of transition and change;

—suggest principles and guidelines for organizational reform together with some applications of them by way of illustration;

—insist on the widest possible participation in whatever kind of reform that is attempted; consultation must be broad and public if the real life of the Church is to be involved;

—promote the new structures, suggested by the Council and hardly tried, so that we might have the benefit of honest and widespread experimentation;

—compile a list of grievances or complaints against the present structures, and then suggest some possible legal remedies; this is the common law mode of procedure.

The discussions of these disparate alternatives was lively, warm, and protracted. The position paper, "Towards Constitutional Development Within the Church" is the product of the consensus which emerged.

Notes on

Constitutional Development

Peter Huizing, S. J.

There has been and there still is much talk and writing about a Constitution of the Church. Attempts have been made to draft such a Constitution, even officially. Some people strongly hold that there should be a fundamental law of the universal Church, a set of rules which would contain the basic outlines of the structure of ecclesiastical society and its government. It has even been suggested that this Church Constitution should be a description of the divine law, the *ius divinum*, given by Christ Himself to the Church.

In the papers, discussions and resolutions of the New York Symposium held on October 7, 8 and 9, 1967, the idea of outlining divine laws is completely absent. Probably because the assembly instinctively felt that no ecclesiastical institution whatsoever, be it the papacy or the episcopate or the sacraments, could be, in its ever developing concrete historical existence, wholly and only "divine." For example, the divine institution of papal primacy existed in Peter, in Damasus and Leo I, in Gregory I and Gregory VII, in Boniface VIII and in Alexander VI, as it exists in Paul VI; but the same institution appears to be very different in those different popes. Nor would it be quite easy to find out what exactly is the divine

Father Peter Huizing, S.J., is a professor of Canon Law at the University of Nijmegen, Holland, and a lecturer at the University of Louvain, Belgium. He is former dean of the faculty of Canon Law at the Gregorian University, Rome, and is a specialist in the history of law and in the matrimonial law of the Church. He is one of the consultants to the Commission for Revision of Canon Law.

nucleus within all those different historical appearances. It even is questionable if this divine nucleus itself is not historically changeable.

Apparently the Symposium felt no need to draft a Schema for a written Constitution of the Church. Sound and lasting Constitutions, as history proves, have been made when the structures of government of a nation and its institutions have reached a certain level of stability. Constitutions created in times of revolution or strong evolution have all disappeared as soon as they were invented. The Catholic Church, now in a period of rapid development, could hardly pretend to have a better change for a durable written Constitution.

What is needed now is to find structures and institutions capable of carrying out in practice the principles laid down by Vatican Council II. A new Church order will have to apply in practice the principles of collegiality, subsidiarity, personal responsibility and freedom of Catholics, ecumenism, religious freedom, unity of the universal Church in a variety of local churches, openness towards the Secular City, and much else. And all that in order to fulfill the essential Christian mission in the world today, to be a living sign of Christ's redemption of mankind.

The New York Symposium thought the best thing it could do was precisely to suggest concrete ways to realize the aims of the Council. Moreover, it was firmly convinced that this work cannot be done by canonists and theologians only, but needs the collaboration of all human sciences that have anything to say about society and its organization. Without the contribution of our best human social values there seems to be little hope that a Church order would be a valuable instrument to further the divine values of the Church. It felt that a cleancut written Constitution would be of little help and even a dangerous framework. So it tried only to formulate a few suggestions that seemed to be of some importance for a real constitutional development within the Church along the broad lines given by the Council. It is not amazing that its work is far from complete; that most or perhaps all the conclusions need still further discussion. What is amazing is that so much could have been accomplished in so short a time.

However, I feel that what is really new and most important, is the very approach to the problem of Church Constitution adopted by this Symposium. It is this approach, prior to the discussion on any particular topic, that will have to be taken into serious consideration by all who are interested in a realistic constitutional development of the Catholic Church.

II.

THE PRESENT SITUATION

Present Organizational Design

and Structure of the

Roman Catholic Church

Edward Heston, C. S. C.

It is hardly necessary to point out that the government of the Roman Catholic Church is "pyramidal," in the sense that all authority is summed up in and leads to the Pope. The Bishop of Rome is the *visible* head of the Church; Christ Himself is its one, *invisible* head. Strictly speaking, there is only one Head of the Church, namely Christ Jesus, and the Pope is His representative. By the Lord Jesus the Pope is invested with a primacy of authority, in and through Peter. The Pope is Peter visible in the Church today, continuing in the world the exercise of the primacy which Peter received from Christ on the shores of the Sea of Galilee. (Math. 16, 18-19).

It cannot be forgotten that not a few aspects of the understanding and the exercise of papal authority in the Roman Catholic Church stem from the fact that from an early age and even until less than a century ago, this spiritual power co-existed and was co-exercised with temporal power in the strict sense of the term. The Popes were temporal rulers like many of their counterparts in Europe and it was only natural, though also

Father Edward L. Heston, C.S.C., is the Procurator General of the Congregation of Holy Cross, and has been resident in Rome for several years. He is a consultor to the Congregation for Religious. He is the author of THE HOLY SEE AT WORK, *one of the few books describing the function of the Roman congregations and offices. During the Second Vatican Council Father Heston achieved distinction for his splendid liaison work with the English-speaking news media.*

regrettable, that the exercise of their authority should in many things have followed along the lines of what was then regarded as proper for temporal rulers

1 / The Pope

In the Bishop of Rome is vested the fullness of authority, legislative, executive and judicial, in the Roman Catholic Church. The First Vatican Council (1869-1870) defined the dogma of the personal infallibility of the Roman Pontiff. According to this definition, in the exercise of his supreme teaching office in the field of faith and morals, the Pope, by a special divine charism, is safeguarded against the possibility of error when explicitly and authoritatively defining a specific point of belief or morality.

Canon 218 of the Code of Canon Law declares that the Roman Pontiff, the Successor of St. Peter in the primacy, is endowed not only with a primacy of honor but with supreme and full jurisdictional power over the entire Church, both in matters pertaining to faith and morals and in those touching on the discipline and government of the Church spread throughout the entire world. The canon then describes distinctly the nature of this power: it is genuinely episcopal, flows directly from the papal office (i.e. it is *ordinary* jurisdiction), touches immediately each and every Church, each and every pastor and every one of the faithful, and is absolutely independent of any and all human authority.

Hence it is naturally within the authority of the Pope to legislate for the entire Church. Strictly speaking, if he so wishes, the Pope can act alone. However, it is hardly to be expected that any Pope, especially in modern times, would be so imprudent as to act without seeking competent advice. Nevertheless, there is no provision for any kind of parliament in the Church; there is no *obligatory* consultation. It is true that the Sacred College of Cardinals is sometimes called the "Senate of the Pope," but this is more of an analogy than anything else. The Cardinals have *no right to be consulted*. It has been said somewhat facetiously that, whereas the Pope can do anything at all without the Cardinals, all the Cardinals can do without the Pope is to elect a new Pope!

Neither is there any strict obligation on the part of the Pope to consult the bishops of the world. Even with the concept of collegiality as clarified and proclaimed by the recent Vatican Council II, the college of bishops cannot function without its head, which is the Pope.

The principal is that *no* college is complete without its Head. Hence the bishops of the Church can never oblige the Pope to act nor can they prevent him from acting.

The Pope's usual *administrative* arm is the Roman Curia, about which more later.

2 / The Bishops

Canon 329, paragraph 1, thus describes the position of individual bishops in the Church: They are the successors of the apostles and, by divine institution, are placed in charge of their particular churches, which they govern by ordinary power, i.e. by power flowing from their office, and under the authority of the Roman Pontiff. This canon does away with an image of bishops which prevailed at times in the past, according to which bishops were regarded as hardly more than messenger-boys of the Pope, receiving their power from and through him, having no authority of their own except in whatever the Pope was unable or unwilling to do directly by himself.

It is important that this canon declares the divine institution of the episcopate. This means that the existence of the episcopate is not dependent on the whim or caprice of an individual Pope. There is no question but that the Pope can remove individual bishops from their Sees, or even all the bishops of an area or a nation. This has happened in some instances. Nevertheless, no Pope could undertake to do away with bishops entirely throughout the Church, with the intention of governing personally through individual and personal representatives or through a parliament. Thus the present Canon Law recognizes in each bishop a genuine personality, which is gradually becoming still clearer in the light of Vatican II. The bishop is invested with the right and the duty to govern his diocese both in spiritualities and in temporalities, with legislative, judicial and coercive power to be exercised conformably to the norms of Canon Law (can. 335, paragraph 1).

Bishops are legislators, each in his own diocese. There is a parallel here with the position of the Pope. The bishop is, strictly speaking, supreme in his diocese. There is no *legislative* body to assist him. Any of the special groups now being organized—clerical senates, lay advisory organizations and the like—have purely consultative functions. Even in a diocesan Synod, which is attended by a good cross-section of the clergy

31

and religious of the diocese, the bishop is the *sole legislator* and only he signs and promulgates the Synodal Constitutions and Decrees (Can. 362).

Laws enacted by bishops must be in accord with the common law of the entire Church. Such laws may never be in conflict with the common law (contra jus), although they may provide for cases or situations not envisioned in the law (praeter jus). Up to the recent Council, Bishops, according to canon 336, paragraph 1, could dispense from the common law of the Church only in urgent cases, when recourse to Rome was impossible and there was at the same time question of laws in which the Holy See usually dispenses without difficulty. (can. 81). Since Vatican II, the Bishops' powers of relaxing universal laws of the Church have been greatly broadened. Now they can act in cases where the good of one or more souls is involved and provided that the decision in a particular field has not been explicitly reserved to himself by the Roman Pontiff. The Pope has published the list of these specific cases.

3 / Ecumenical Councils

The attention of the world was recently greatly taken up with the meeting and the subsequent decisions of the Second Ecumenical Vatican Council. An Ecumenical Council is a traditional element in the legislative framework of the Church, although the infrequency of Councils has tended to keep their importance somewhat in the background. The Code of Canon Law sums up briefly, more or less as follows, the basic principles regarding Ecumenical Councils and their place in the legislative structure of the Church.

In the first place, an Ecumenical Council is not a higher authority to which individuals or groups may appeal against decisions of the Roman Pontiff. There can be no Ecumenical Council which has not been convoked by the Bishop of Rome. It is likewise the right of the Roman Pontiff to preside over an Ecumenical Council, either personally or through Legates, to determine the agenda and the procedure to be followed, to transfer the meetings of the Council to another place, as also to suspend it, to dissolve it, and to confirm its decrees (Can. 222).

The following are members of an Ecumenical Council and in it enjoy the right of suffrage:

1) the Cardinals of the Church, even though they be not

bishops (this provision is no longer in force, in view of what appears to be the established practice of elevating to the episcopal dignity all non-bishops appointed to the Sacred College of Cardinals);

2) patriarchs, primates, residential archbishops and bishops, even though not yet consecrated;

3) abbots or prelates having territorial jurisdiction (abbates and praelati nullius);

4) the Abbot-Primate of a monastic order, Abbots-Presidents of monastic Congregations and the Superiors General of exempt clerical institutes, but not of other religious institutes unless other provisions have been stated in the decree of convocation;

5) titular bishops who are called to the Council have deliberative vote in the Council, unless the contrary is expressly declared in the convocation.

Theologians and experts in canon law who may have been invited to the Council have only consultative vote (Can. 223).

Anyone summoned to the Council in keeping with the preceeding provision must be present. If detained by a legitimate impediment, he is to send a proxy and justify his absence. A proxy who is one of the Council Fathers does not thereby acquire a double vote. If the proxy is not a Council Father, he can take part only in the Public Sessions but has no right to vote. Upon the conclusion of the Council, the proxy has the right to sign the acts (Can. 224).

The Council Fathers are empowered to add other questions to the agenda proposed by the Roman Pontiff, provided they have previously obtained the assent of the presiding officer of the Council (Can. 226).

Council decrees, etc., have no definitive binding force until they have confirmed by the Roman Pontiff and have been promulgated by his order. (Can. 227).

An Ecumenical Council exercises supreme jurisdiction over the entire Church, but only when working in conjunction with the Roman Pontiff (Can. 228).

Should the Roman Pontiff die while a Council is in session, the Council is thereby automatically suspended until the new Pope orders its resumption and continuation.

4 / General Principles on Ecclesiastical Laws

Laws can be enacted by those authorities in the Church who are empowered to do so: the Pope for the entire Church, bishops for their individual dioceses, and certain other Superiors of ecclesiastical or religious bodies. No particular form is prescribed for the enactment of a law. All laws are enacted when they are promulgated (Can. 8, paragraph 1). The general principle laid down in canon 8, paragraph 2, is that laws are not presumed to be personal, but rather territorial, unless the contrary is stated. Laws enacted by the Apostolic See are promulgated by their publication in the official publication *Acta Apostolicae Sedis,* (Acts of the Apostolic See), unless in particular cases some other method is prescribed. They go into effect three months from the date of the issue of the *Acta* in which they have appeared, unless by their very nature or in the text of the new law, a shorter or longer period has been especially and expressly stated. This delay is known as the "vacatio legis" and is intended to provide time for knowledge of the law to become common and for its preliminary uncertainties to be clarified before it becomes obligatory (Can. 9). As for the interpretation of laws, only the legislator or his successor, or those to whom this authority has been entrusted, may give an authentic and binding interpretation of the law (Can. 17, paragraph 1). At times, while awaiting an authentic interpretation from competent authority, other superiors in the Church may issue disciplinary interpretations binding on those whom the law obliges until such time as an authentic interpretation is forthcoming. Laws enacted in order to forestall a general danger are binding even though in a particular case the danger in question is not present (Can. 21). A later law enacted by competent authority does away with a previous law if this is expressly stated or is in direct contradiction to it, or if it undertakes to completely reorganize the whole matter. But a general law does not interfere with legislation affecting special places or individual persons unless it is so expressly stated (Can. 22). In case of doubt the revocation of a previously existing law is not presumed, but later laws are to be interpreted in the light of previous laws and, insofar as possible, are to be reconciled with them (Can. 23).

5 / The Roman Curia

A. *In general:*
Canon 7 states that by the "Apostolic See" is understood not only the Roman Pontiff but also, unless a different interpretation is clear from the circumstances or the context,

those Congregations, Tribunals and Offices through which the same Roman Pontiff usually dispatches the business of the Church Universal. According to Can. 242, the Roman Curia is composed of the Congregations, Tribunals and Offices described in the subsequent canons.

"Curia" is an ancient Latin term signifying a center of government, a Senate-hall, a place for court sessions. It has with the passage of time acquired a special ecclesiastical significance not always restricted to the "Roman Curia," since we speak also of a Diocesan Curia and even of the headquarters of a religious institute as a Curia, for example, the Jesuit Curia in Roma. The Roman Curia is an ecclesiastical counterpart of "official Washington."

Although the earliest origins of the Roman Curia go back to the first beginnings of the Church, its present-day organization reflects basically the reform introduced by Pope Sixtus V on January 22, 1588, and later modified substantially by Pope St. Pius X on June 29, 1908. The two reforms have given us the general structure which characterizes the Roman Curia today. A more immediate updating of the Curia is now in the making.

The purpose of the Curia is to aid the Pope in the government of the Universal Church. The individual Congregations, Tribunals, and Offices are to follow the general and specific norms laid down by the Pope (Can. 243, paragraph 1). They are to undertake nothing of special importance without the Holy Father being advised thereof by the competent superiors of the Congregations, Tribunals, or Offices (Can. 244). The Curia does not act on its own authority. Whatever it does is done with jurisdiction conferred on it by the Pope through special or extraordinary faculties. In many instances the final decision on important matters must be approved by the Holy Father personally. Each Congregation, Tribunal and Office operates independently, according to its specific competence, as determined in Canon Law (Canons 246-264). During the vacancy of the Holy See, the various units of the Curia continue their ordinary operations in routine matters, but cannot take any decisions beyond ordinary routine administration. There is no such thing as the "Roman Curia" acting as a unit or a block. It does not act independently but, either directly or indirectly always under the supervision of the Roman Pontiff, as stated above, nor as a unit. In fact, there is sometimes a regrettable lack of coordination among the units.

It cannot be said that any one method of work is consistently

35

followed in all the various sectors of the Roman Curia. As is only natural, the procedures observed in Tribunals and Offices will be quite different from those followed in the Congregations, and this because of the different nature of the matters under discussion. But it can be said that, in generic fashion, the Congregations particularly work along pretty much the same lines.

Strictly speaking, whether there be question of Congregations, Tribunals, or Offices, the only members in the strict sense are the Cardinals assigned to the various units either at the time of their elevation to the Sacred College or later. However, the term "Congregation," "Tribunal" or "Office" generally includes the entire staff, of all those having a part in its ordinary operative functioning.

Usually each Congregation is in charge of a Cardinal Prefect, a Secretary and an Under-Secretary. The Prefects correspond pretty much to our Cabinet Secretaries in Washington. In those Congregations whose prefecture is reserved to the Pope personally, the Cardinal in charge is known as "Pro-Prefect," a term which is more or less equivalent to "Acting Prefect." According to the volume of its business, each Congregation will operate under a group of lesser officials. There exists for each Congregation a larger number of Consultors, or experts, who are called in for the study of various problems. Sometimes they do their work individually; at others they work in groups, according to the directives of responsible authorities in the Congregation. The work of the Consultors is usually then discussed in a special commission. The findings of the commission are referred for discussion in a *congresso* of the Congregation, which is a meeting of all of the officials, under the presidency of the Cardinal Prefect. Most matters will be decided in this way and then, if necessary, referred to the Holy Father. Important matters may go through still another phase, which is the Plenary Meeting of all the Cardinals attached to the Congregation. Very important items will then be taken by the Cardinal Prefect to audience with the Holy Father for ultimate decision. Although, barring a particular commission from the Holy Father, the Congregations of the Roman Curia do not of themselves enjoy legislative power, they may nevertheless take the lead in initiating programs which they regard as useful and profitable to the Church. Examples of this can be found in the role played, for instance, by the Sacred Congregation of Religious in launching some seventeen years ago, the great movement of "aggiornamento" in the religious life, and in favoring the program which was first organized in the United States to insure the proper formation of sisters along religious, educational and professional lines. As another instance, we could refer to the Sacred Congregation of the Council and the organization of special catechetical institutes and programs in various countries. A growing trend towards decentralization is expected to reduce notably the amount of detail work now depending on Curia action in Rome.

B. *In particular:*

The following is a breif account of the competence and nature of each of the Congregations, Tribunals and Offices constituting the Roman Curia:

The SACRED CONGREGATION FOR THE DOCTRINE OF THE FAITH, formerly known as the Holy Office, has as Prefect the Pope himself and has the task of safeguarding faith and morals. It has judicial power on whatever offenses are reserved to it under its own proper rules and regulations, with authority to judge criminal cases not only on appeal from the Tribunal of the Local Ordinary, but also in first instance, if the case is taken to the Congregation directly. It has exclusive authority over everything pertaining directly or indirectly to the Pauline Privilege and to the matrimonial impediments of Disparity of Worship and Mixed Religion. Consequently, all questions on these matters must be submitted to this Congregation which, if it so wishes, may refer them to another Congregation (e.g. that of the Sacraments) or to the Tribunal of the Sacred Roman Rota (Can. 247).

This Congregation formerly had the responsibility for examining books submitted to it for suspect doctrine and, if necessary, condemning them. In the recent re-organization of this Sacred Congregation and the subsequent disappearance of the "Index of Forbidden Books" and of the prohibition of books as a matter of ecclesiastical law, this function is no longer exercised. The re-organization also provided for a special "College of Lawyers for the Defense," a group of ecclesiastics to whom persons brought before the Holy Office in criminal trial may apply for defense. Formerly, one individual had the title of "Advocate of the Accused" but the exercise of this function was more or less a formality. The designation of individuals from different areas of the world indicates that any such trials in the future will pay much more consideration than in the past to the defense of the accused. The Advocates designated are from Italy, Poland, France, Spain, and the United States.

The SACRED CONSISTORIAL CONGREGATION is next in dignity and importance and also has the Pope as Prefect. Among its ex officio members are the Cardinal Prefect of the Congregation of Seminaries and

Universities, and the Secretary of State. Among its Consultors are always found the Secretary of the Holy Office, the Secretary of the Congregation of Extraordinary Ecclesiastical Affairs, as well as the Secretary of the Congregation of Seminaries and Universities. This Congregation had as its task in ancient times to prepare matters for discussion in Consistories and likewise, outside of territories under the Sacred Congregation for the Propagation of the Faith, it sees to the erection of new dioceses and ecclesiastical provinces and also to the division of existing dioceses. It proposes ecclesiastics for appointment as bishops (Ordinaries, Co-adjutors or Auxiliaries) after carrying out the canonical investigation on the qualifications of all candidates. This Congregation supervises the general status of dioceses. It keeps watch over the fulfillment of the duties binding upon Ordinaries, studies the reports sent in by bishops on their respective dioceses, and also decides on apostolic visitations of dioceses in case they are regarded as necessary or useful (Can. 248).

The SACRED CONGREGATION FOR THE DISCIPLINE OF THE SACRAMENTS has responsibility for all the legislation on the Seven Sacraments, without prejudice to the rights of the Congregation for the Doctrine of the Faith on doctrinal questions and the authority of the Sacred Congregation of Rites for the ritual and the ceremonies to be observed in confecting, administering and receiving the Sacraments. The Sacred Congregation likewise has exclusive competence over the discipline of marriage, as also that of all the other Sacraments, as well as the celebration of the Eucharistic Sacrifice, with the exception of points reserved to other Congregations. It likewise has exclusive authority over the dissolution of non-consummated marriage and passes judgment on the existence and the sufficiency of the causes alleged for the granting of this dispensation. If it prefers, it may refer the study of these details to the Sacred Roman Rota. Likewise this Congregation studies all questions touching the validity of marriage but can also send these questions on to the competent Tribunal for more accurate investigation and study. It likewise judges all questions concerning the obligations annexed to major orders and examines all questions arising on the validity of sacred ordination (Can. 249). It should be remarked here that since 1964, all requests for release from priestly obligations, are reserved to a special commission working at the Sacred Congregation for the Doctrine of the Faith.

To the SACRED CONGREGATION OF THE COUNCIL belong all matters pertaining to the discipline of the secular clergy and the Christian people. It sees to the observance of the laws of Christian life, and is enpowered to dispense the faithful from the observance of these laws. It is in charge of matters dealing with parish priests, canons and pious sodalities. It has jurisdiction over all pious bequests, pious works, Mass stipends, ecclesiastical goods, diocesan taxes etc. It has the power to decide on a compromise with those in illegal possession of ecclesiastical goods, even those belonging to religious, and likewise to permit the faithful to acquire ecclesiastical goods which may have been usurped by civil authority. It has authority over whatever pertains to the celebration and the approval of Councils and to assemblies or conferences of bishops, outside territories under the Sacred Congregation for the Propagation of the Faith. The Congregation of the Council handles all controversies referred to it, if in its judgment these can be decided administratively; otherwise it refers them to the competent tribunal (Can. 250). It conducts a part time school with practical experience for training future diocesan officials.

The SACRED CONGREGATION OF RELIGIOUS has authority over everything touching the government, discipline, studies, property and privileges of religious of both sexes, whether of solemn or of simple vows, and likewise of all those who live in community after the manner of religious, but without vows, as also of secular Third Orders, without prejudice to the rights of the Congregation for the Propagation of the Faith. Consequently, referring all judicial questions to the competent Tribunal and without prejudice to the rights of the Sacred Congregation for the Doctrine of the Faith and the Sacred Congregation of the Council in their respective fields, this Congregation handles all questions administratively, but if the dispute is between a religious and a non-religious, then, especially at the request of the parties, the Sacred Congregation can refer the matter to another Congregation or to a competent Tribunal. Lastly this Congregation is empowered to grant all dispensations from common law for religious, without prejudice to the authority of the Congregation for the Doctrine of the Faith (Can. 251). In recent times there has been a move to change the title of the Congregation because its authority extends to some organizations, such as Secular Institutes whose members are not "religious" in the juridical sense of the term. The Sacred Congregation has a special school for the preparation of experts in the Canon Law on Religious.

The SACRED CONGREGATION FOR THE PROPAGATION OF THE FAITH directs missions for the preaching of the Gospel and the teaching of Catholic doctrine. It trains necessary ministers and has authority over all matters which in any way affect the mission fields of the Church. It has authority over the celebration and approval of councils in territories under its jurisdiction, i.e., those areas where the Sacred Hierarchy has not yet been erected. To this Congregation are subject likewise those localities, which although the hierarchy may have been erected, are nevertheless regarded as missionary areas. It also supervises societies of ecclesiastics and seminaries founded for the exclusive purpose of engaging in missionary activity, and has special competence over their rules, administration, and the norms governing the ordination of their members. This Congregation must refer to a competent Congregation any matters connected with faith, marriage cases, or the general norms governing sacred rites. This Sacred Congregation has authority over religious for anything touching them as missionaries either as individuals or as a community, but for anything dealing with religious as such, whether as individuals or as communities the Congregation for the Propagation of the Faith must defer to the Congregation of Religious (Can. 252).

The CONGREGATION OF SACRED RITES examines and decides all questions rising from the rites and ceremonies of the Latin Church, with the exception of those dealing only remotely with sacred rites such as rights of seniority and others. Consequently, this Sacred Congregation will see to it that sacred rites and ceremonies are carefully observed in the celebration of Mass, the administration of the Sacraments, the celebration of choral office, in whatever pertains to the worship of the Latin Church. The Congregation grants necessary dispensations and attempts to forestall abuses. Lastly, it has exclusive authority over the beatification and the canonization of Servants of God and over any questions concerning relics (Can. 253).

The authority of the Congregation of Sacred Rites has been somewhat restricted since Vatican II as the result of the organization of the "Supreme Council for the Execution of the Decree on the Sacred Liturgy." At the beginning there was no small amount of friction between the Congregation of Rites and this Supreme Council but a sort of modus vivendi has been worked out whereby all decrees dealing with liturgical changes, though worked out by the Council, are now published over the joint signatures of the Prefect of the Sacred Congregation and the President of the Supreme Council.

The SACRED CEREMONIAL CONGREGATION is in charge of all ceremonies concerned with the Papal Court and with sacred functions performed by Cardinals outside the papal chapel. It likewise has the last word on questions of precedence among Cardinals and among the Ambassadors accredited to the Holy See (Can. 254). It might be compared to a civil government's Protcal Office.

The SACRED CONGREGATION FOR EXTRAORDINARY ECCLESIAS-TICAL AFFAIRS has the task of erecting and dividing dioceses and of proposing candidates for episcopal appointments as often as these appointments must be discussed with civil governments because of diplomatic relations or special agreements. This Congregation likewise studies whatever matters are submitted to it by the Sovereign Pontiff through the Cardinal-Secretary of State, particularly in problems arising from the civil legislation of various nations and the implementation of Concordats and other reciprocal agreements (Can. 255).

The SACRED CONGREGATION FOR SEMINARIES AND UNIVER-SITIES is the competent authority for everything pertaining to the discipline, government, temporal administration and the program of studies in seminaries, without prejudice to the rights of the Sacred Congregation for the Propagation of the Faith for its own proper territories. It could be looked upon as a Department of Education. It likewise watches over the government and the studies in Faculties or other institutions dependent on Church authority, including those directed by religious institutes. It examines and approves new foundations, grants authorization to confer academic degrees and determines the norms to be followed. Among the members of this Congregation are, among others, the Cardinal Pro-Prefect of the Consistorial Congregation, with the Secretary of the Sacred Congregation being regularly among its Consultors (Can. 256). The Vatican Council II decree on Priestly Formation, *Optatam totius,* has greatly limited the authority of this Sacred Congregation by determining that the details of seminary formation are henceforth the responsibility of individual National Episcopal Conferences. Thus the overall direction of seminary programs throughout the world will be greatly decentralized.

The SACRED CONGREGATION FOR THE EASTERN CHURCHES is presided over by the Roman Pontiff. To this Congregation are reserved all matters involving persons, the discipline, the rites of the Eastern Churches, even if these questions are in some way connected with persons of the Latin Rite. Hence this Congregation exercises over all Eastern Rite Churches whatever authority has been granted to other Congregations for the Churches of the Latin Rite, without prejudice to the jurisdiction of the Sacred Congregation for the Doctrine of the Faith. This Congregation decides questions administratively. Should there be question of a problem to be handled by judicial process, then it shall be turned over to another Tribunal, as decided by the Congregation (Can. 257).

The fields of authority of the *Tribunals* of the Roman Curia are summed up as follows:

The SACRED PENITENTIARY is a Tribunal dealing exclusively with the internal forum, that is to say, with doubts and questions of conscience, whether in connection with or independently of the Sacrament of Penance. Its presiding officer is a Cardinal, known as the "Major Penitentiary." This Congregation grants favors only for the internal forum, as also absolutions, dispensations, commutations, sanations, condonations, and it likewise has the authority to study and to decide cases of conscience. It passes judgment on the use and the granting of indulgences, without prejudice to the rights of the Sacred Congregation for the Doctrine of the Faith as regards either the dogmatic aspects of indulgences or the introduction of new prayers and devotions (Can. 258).

Some basic principles should be summarized before any discussion of the two Tribunals of the Holy See which deal with the external forum. According to the provisions of Can. 1569, paragraph 1, because of the primacy of the Roman Pontiff, every member of the faithful anywhere in the world has the right to bring to the Holy See any judicial or criminal case, in any stage of judgment and at any phase of the discussion, and to have the matter judged by its supreme authority. Consequently, for the entire Catholic world, the Roman Pontiff is the Supreme Judge, deciding matters either himself personally, through a Tribunal set up by him, or by judges delegated by him (Can. 1597).

The ordinary Tribunal of the Holy See for cases on appeal is the SACRED ROMAN ROTA, which is a collegiate Tribunal composed of a certain number of Auditors presided over by a Dean, who is the first among equals. These Auditors must be at least doctors in both Canon and Roman law. The appointment of Auditors of the Rota is reserved to the Roman Pontiff. The Sacred Rota judges cases either through rotating groups of three Auditors or in plenary session, unless in a particular case the Sovereign Pontiff has decided otherwise (Can. 1598). Its role and functions closely resemble those of the United States Supreme Court.

The Sacred Rota judges in second instance i.e., on first appeal, any cases already judged in first instance by any local tribunal, and which have been brought to the Holy See by legitimate appeal, because no judicial case is regarded as definitely settled until it has received two conforming verdicts from two different courts. It also judges in first instance cases reserved to it in this phase by law or which the Holy Father may have seen fit to refer to it directly. Administrative decisions by Local Ordinaries cannot be appealed to the Roman Rota but recourse against them is reserved exclusively to the competent Sacred Congregation (Can. 1599 and Can. 1601). The Rota conducts a specialized training school for its own future lawyers and for legal experts on the diocesan level.

The Supreme Tribunal of the Apostolic Signature is composed of several Cardinals, one of whom has the title of Prefect. It is a court of appeal from sentences of the Rota, but it should be pointed out that it is not empowered to judge the merits of cases legitimately decided by the Rota. It passes judgment only on violations of the judicial secret and on damages eventually caused by Auditors of the Sacred Roman Rota as the result of a null or unjust act. It judges any accusation of suspicion lodged against an Auditor of the Rota. It is competent to decide disputes over competence between lower Tribunals and also determines by delegated power, whether a petition should be honored to permit causes to be discussed in first instance by the Roman Rota (Can. 1603). It has no counterpart in the American judicial system.

There are four "Offices" of the Roman Curia. The first is the APOSTOLIC CHANCERY, presided over by the Cardinal Chancellor of Holy Roman Church. Its proper office is to prepare Apostolic Letters or Bulls for appointment to benefices and to consistorial offices, such as bishoprics, as well as those dealing with the erection of new provinces, dioceses etc. These Letters or Bulls are sent out only after authorization has been received from the Sacred Consistorial Congregation, or by mandate from the Sovereign Pontiff, with due observance in individual cases of the terms of the particular mandate (Can. 260).

The APOSTOLIC DATARY is the Office which in ancient times, had the duty of dating documents. It was an important office because dates very often determine the validity of acts allegedly based on documents. The Datary is headed by a Cardinal, and has competence to pass judgment on the fitness of candidates for non-consistorial benefices reserved to the Apostolic See. It likewise conducts all business involved in such appointments (Can. 261). Because its practical usefulness today is almost nil, it is expected to disappear in the re-organization of the Curia.

The APOSTOLIC CAMERA is directed by the Cardinal Camerlengo of the Holy Roman Church and is entrusted with the care and administration of property and the temporal rights of Rome. During this period the Apostolic Camera is to observe carefully the rules laid down by St.

Pius X in his special Constitution on the vacancy of the Holy See, issued on December 25, 1904 (Can. 262). Actually this office has lost practically all its importance because the administration of the temporalities of the Holy See has been vested in two or three specialized offices organized in recent times precisely for this purpose. The "Administration of the Goods of the Holy See," which is like a Vatican Finance Ministry, and the "Special Administration of the Goods of the Holy See" for the funds paid to the Vatican by the government of Italy in 1929 as compensation for property seized in 1870.

The Office of the SECRETARIAT OF STATE is in charge of the Cardinal Secretary of State. It is composed of three parts. The First Section is under the Secretary of the Congregation for Extraordinary Ecclesiastical Affairs, and deals with matters turned over to it for study by the Sovereign Pontiff. It refers to the respective Sacred Congregations anything falling within their competence. The Second Section, under the Substitute or Under-Secretary of State, despatches ordinary business. The Third Section is in charge of the Chancellor of Apostolic Briefs and sees to the preparation of Apostolic Briefs (Can. 263).

The Secretariat of Briefs to Princes and the Secretariat of Latin Letters have the special task of composing in Latin the documents turned over to them for preparation by the Sovereign Pontiff (Can. 264).

6 / Nuncios and Delegates

Strictly speaking, the representatives of the Holy See in various countries, whether Apostolic Nuncios, that is to say enjoying diplomatic status and accreditation to the government or whether they be simply Apostolic Delegates, that is to say, accredited to the hierarchy of the country without diplomatic rank, play no role in the legislative organization of the Church. If their duties are restricted to what we in find in canon law, the task of Apostolic Delegates, canon 267, paragraph 2 states that their one ordinary power is to keep watch over the territory assigned to them and over the various churches there and to report thereon to the Roman Pontiff. However, the passage of time and the development of new situations has been responsible for Apostolic Nuncios and Delegates becoming real liaisons between the Church in various countries and the Holy See. This has been true because the Holy See has seen fit to confer special powers and faculties on Nuncios and Delegates in order to facilitate recourse to the Holy See. Not infrequently Nuncios and Delegates are appealed to by individuals or groups, whether religious or lay, against the provisions of higher local superiors. As mentioned earlier, strictly speaking, neither the Nuncio nor the Delegate would have any strict authority to *decide* any such questions. He would, however, interpose his good offices in an attempt to bring about an amicable understanding or, if all such good efforts failed, he would then refer the matter to the Holy See for final adjudication.

7 / The Synod of Bishops

By a Motu Proprio entitled "Apostolica Sollicitudo," dated September 15, 1965, Pope Paul VI erected for the first time a Synod of Bishops, whose function it would be to provide all the bishops of the Catholic world with a clearer and more effective means of sharing in the solicitude of the Bishop of Rome for the universal Church. Thus the organization of this Synod was a direct outgrowth of the acceptance by the Second Vatican Council of the doctrine of the collegiality of the episcopate, that is to say, the doctrine which declares that all bishops of the Church share with the Pope, their Supreme and Visible Head, and never without him, authority and responsibility for the government of the entire Church. The Synod of Bishops is a central ecclesiastical institution, representing the entire Catholic episcopate. It will have the specific task to inform and give advice, and can have deliberative power whenever such power is conferred on it by the Sovereign Pontiff. In such cases, the Pope will always confirm the decisions of the Synod. The Synod can be convoked in general, extraordinary or special meeting. For a general meeting of the Synod the members are, in large part, elected by the various National Episcopal Conferences, and to them will be added ten Religious elected by the Roman Union of Superiors General. The only Cardinals who will be automatically members of the Synod of Bishops will be those in charge of the dicasteries of the Roman Curia. A synod convoked in general meeting will be composed of approximately 190 members. Bishops are elected according to the ratio of one bishop for each twenty-five bishops in the country, but no country may have more than four representatives in the Synod. The Pope may appoint additional members, but not beyond 15% of the total membership. The work of the Synod is organized by a Permanent Secretary, and each Synod will have its own Particular Secretary. Both Secretaries are to be appointed by the Sovereign Pontiff. It must be stressed that the Synod of Bishops has no legislative power independent of that of the Pope. It is purely and simply an advisory body unless in some special case the Pope confers on it legislative authority. History's first Synod of Bishops of the Roman Catholic Church opened in Rome on September 29, 1967.

8 / National Episcopal Conferences

The Council Decree on the Pastoral Duties of Bishops recognizes as legitimate juridical entities in Church government the National Conferences of Bishops, which had already been in existence in some countries, in varying degrees of organization and authority. The Council has declared that no National Conference of Bishops will have authority to impose its decisions indiscriminately on all the bishops of a country. The National Conferences will have juridical power to demand conformity only in those cases in which such authority has been conferred on them by the Holy See, e.g., in the implementation of the provisions of the Constitution on the Sacred Liturgy, and others which may be determined subsequently. In all other cases, the decisions of the National Conferences will have for the bishops of the country only an advisory value. It is expected that the coming revision of the Code of Canon Law will turn over to the respective National Conferences of Bishops the determination of not a few of the details which are now taken care of in the various canons of the Code.

9 / The Code of Canon Law

Until the present time, the law of the Church has been expressed in the 2,414 canons of the Code of Canon Law. Coming as the result of long years of work which were an answer to the long standing plea that the laws of the Church be simplified by being summed up in a "Code," and not left laying around, so to speak, in various different documents and collections, the Code of Canon Law was promulgated by Pope Benedict XV in 1917, and went into effect on Pentecost Sunday, 1918. With some changes in minor points it has remained the law of the Church up to the present time. Official and authentic interpretation of the meaning of the canons was entrusted to the Pontifical Commission for the Interpretation of the Code of Canon Law.

The Code of Canon Law follows the general outlines and basic principles of Roman Law, adapted to the needs of an ecclesiastical society. It is composed of five books: I-General Norms; II-Persons; III-Things; IV-Juridical Procedure; V-Crimes and Punishments. It undertakes to determine many details of the life of the Church and this on a universal scale, the only exception being that the canons do not apply to the Churches of the Eastern Rites unless this follows from the nature of the canon or is otherwise clearly stated (Can. 1).

There has been much discussion in favor of changing the structure of the law of the Church, so that it will not reflect what many regard as a now out-moded approach to the life and activities of the members of the Church. There has been much talk of elaborating a Constitution of the Church, based on the doctrine found in Scripture and in the teaching magisterium of the Church, and containing only those principles which are of divine law and which, consequently, will never change. The determination of details would then be left to legislation from the Episcopal Synod, to decisions by National Conferences of Bishops in order to make more allowance for local differences, or, by special mandate from the Pope, to the competent Sacred Congregations of the Roman Curia. It may be that the days of universal determination even of details in a universally binding code of laws are gone forever.

The Reformed Roman Curia

Giancarlo Zizola

With the Apostolic Constitution "Regimini Ecclesiae Universae," published on the 15 August 1967, the Roman Curia has been given a new structure. Paul VI has laid the foundation for making it less Roman and more universal, less clerical and more sacerdotal, less administrative and more pastoral. One of the most pressing demands of the Council has thus been fulfilled. It also maintains the promise which Paul VI made to the cardinals, prelates, and functionaries of the Curia when (in the course of a speech made on September 21, 1963) he astonished them by saying: "It is not only easy to foresee that some reforms will have to be introduced in the Roman Curia; they are indeed much to be desired." Alluding to the criticisms which had been widely made, even in the Council (which at the time of the speech was about to re-assemble for its second session), he then added: "Rome has no need to defend itself by turning a deaf ear to the suggestions made by honest voices; all the less, when the voices are those of friends and brothers."

We have here the first attempt in the whole history of the Church to undertake a general reform of the Curia, always provided that

Mr. Giancarlo Zizola, perhaps the most accurate and highly regarded "vaticanologist" on the Italian scene, is a correspondent for several Catholic newspapers. This article is copyrighted by IDO-C, Information Documentation on the Conciliar Church. Reproduction in whole or in part is strictly forbidden without permission in writing.

one gives the word "reform" its true significance. All the same, however epoch-making the Pope's decision may be, this does not mean that it has succeeded in avoiding the compromises inherent in the actual situation of Church government at this particular moment of the Church's post-conciliar history. But on the eve of the assembly of the Synod of Bishops it was obviously necessary to make the most of the existing circumstances rather than to allow the question to be further postponed.

This consideration helps us to understand the reasons which have led Paul VI to take the reins of the reform into his own hands and to speed up the last phase of the elaboration of the document. The final text shows many signs of this haste, and a number of uncertainties (even in the form) reveal the unresolved conflicts of the preparatory phase, which has lasted for four years and has passed through thirteen successive drafts.

1 / Sixtus V to John XXIII

The machinery of the Roman Curia did not develop on the basis of any one overall principle, but empirically, by "fits and starts" through a long series of additions, definitions, combinations, and changes. Each department of the Church's central government has had a different origin. All of them, moreover, came into being in response to the need of the Popes to have at their disposal some special organisms to provide for the general needs of the Church or the Papal State. According to Nicolò del Re (one of the foremost authorities on this subject), some of the Curial organisms were already in being in the fourth century; but for the most part their development can be dated from the period between the twelfth and sixteenth centuries. Already in 1556, Paul IV had felt the need for more homogeneous structures and had instituted a commission for the reform of the Curia. The reform was carried out by Sixtus V with his famous Apostolic Constitution "Immensa Aeterni Dei," published on the 22 January 1588. It was a wide reform, which brought the number of the "Roman congregations" up to fifteen: six for the administration of the Papal States and nine for the government of the Church.

It was the product of the period immediately following the Council of Trent; i.e. it was Rome's reply to the attacks made upon it by the Reformation and to the need then felt for a central authority capable of preserving Catholic discipline. The new congregations, which were in effect simply commissions of cardinals with particular functions of studying and executing administrative matters, were invested with the powers which had previously belonged to the apostolic chancery and the consistories, where the Pope and the cardinals discussed and decided collegially all the problems connected with the government of the universal Church.[1]

1. THE AMBIGUITY OF THE TWO SOVEREIGNTIES.

The Curia, as constituted by Sixtus V in the period following the Council of Trent, remained substantially unchanged until the beginning of the twentieth century. But already in the eighteenth century the machinery showed signs of cracking. The nepotism which (thanks to the superhuman efforts of Innocent XI and Innocent XII) seemed to have been eliminated, once again came to the surface.

The revolutionary crisis had not made inroads into the system; the papacy had remained anchored to its Italian state and the ambiguity of the co-existence within the pope himself of both temporal and spiritual sovereignty had its repercussions in all the personnel of the Roman Curia, giving an imprint to the duties and activities of its functionaries which at times had very little in common with the evangelical ministry. The central administration of the Church seemed a ponderous archaic apparatus; it had no less than twenty-five "congregations," and an almost equally large number of tribunals, where ecclesiastic and civil matters were disconcertingly mixed; it carried out both judicial and administrative functions, had offices such as the Chancery, the Datary, and the Apostolic Camera, and five specialised secretariats apart from the Secretariat of State, which had become the principal organ of papal government. If one adds to all this the various services of the papal court and the ramifications of the administration of the temporal State, one begins to have an idea of just what "those thousands of parasites interested in the maintenance of the abuses which scandalised Christianity and lent grist to the scorn of the enemies of the Church" [2] must have been like.

2. THE REFORM OF PIUS X

The need for at least a functional reform of the Curia became obvious and inescapable after the loss of the temporal power and

---

1. cf. Nicolo del Re: *La Curia romana*, lineamenti storici-giuridici, (edizioni storia e letteratura, Rome, 1952). The following may also be usefully consulted: Cipriano Calderon, *Iglesia con Pablo VI*, (ediciones Sigueme, Salamanca, 1964), pp. 277-312, containing an ample bibliography of the Roman Curia.
2. cf. Nouvelle Histoire de l'Eglise, IV (Paris, 1966, p. 48)

the strengthening of papal authority effected by the first Vatican Council. This was undertaken by Pius X, who personally supplied the directives for the reform. According to these directives, it was necessary to abolish departments which had become useless and to constitute new ones to meet new needs; to change the names of some of the congregations; to limit the functions of each department; to separate the administrative forum from the purely judicial one; to make a better distribution of work among the various congregations, to avoid duplications, to speed up bureaucratic practices, and to unify the criteria on the basis of which problems were resolved; to apply the principle of official secrecy to all functionaries; to provide the congregations with a consultative body; to regularize the Vatican's economy by unifying "taxes," creating a common fund, and absolutely prohibiting any kind of gift to the officials of the various departments. Pius X was in a hurry. "This is a reform which must be carried out immediately" was his order. Mons. De Lai, a prelate of the Congregation of the Council, sent the first draft to the pope in 1907. Pius X personally developed it into more detailed norms, filling eighteen pages of a copy book. A commission of cardinals was nominated and charged with the task of examining the plan in detail and preparing the executive regulations of the reform. On the 29th June 1908 they were published by Pius X in his *Motu Proprio* entitled "Sapienti Consilio"; they were later incorporated into the Codex of Canon Law prepared under Pius X and promulgated by Benedict XV in 1917.

3. THE ATTITUDE OF PIUS XII

The reform on the whole left the sixteenth-century structure of the Curia unchanged in its general outline. Very soon, however, this structure revealed itself as still less satisfactory, and the need for a further reform was quickly recognized. "I am too old for this" said Pius XI, towards the end of his pontificate, to a cardinal who had proposed he should give the Curia a more up-to-date structure. Pius XII kept a folder with the plans of a reform on his desk for several months. But he could not bring himself to give it the last touches so as to make it workable. Many of his seemingly strange initiatives could, however, be explained in this context. He concentrated power and competence in the Secretariat of State; abandoned personal contacts with the prelates in charge of the various departments, referring them towards the Deputy-Secretary of State or his substitute; he left many positions in the Curia vacant, preferring to nominate "deputy office holders" rather than to make firm appointments.

He received only a very few of the Roman cardinals, whose number diminished in the course of his reign from twenty-seven at the time of his election to twelve at the time of his death. The apparatus of the Curia undoubtedly lost importance during the reign of this somewhat withdrawn pope.

4. THE "INSTITUTIONAL SOLITUDE" OF JOHN XXIII

The approach to the problem changed radically under John XXIII. Great efforts were made in ecclesiology, not simply to regard the Church as based on the papacy, but to understand the papacy in the context of the Church and similarly to conceive the ministry of Peter primarily as a service and only secondly as an authority (and here again as an authority not simply *over* the Church, but rather *within* the Church); i.e., to conceive the primacy of *jurisdiction* as deriving from the primacy of the *faith* (H. Kung).

Pope John was the human incarnation of these theological conquests. Thanks to him, the papacy became a lovable institution in the eyes of those who had once seen it as a scandal or to whom it had continued to be a point of doctrinal controversy, a visible and dogmatic obstacle to ecumenical reconciliation.

It hardly seems worthwhile to ask oneself whether Pope John was also thinking about a reform of the Curia, because this reform sprang from the very circumstances themselves, from the mere fact that a new ecumenical Council had been called. But his efforts to galvanize the Roman Curia into fresh activity after its hibernation during the reign of Pius XII were not sufficient to bring it into the reforming orbit of his pontificate.

During the reign of Pius XII the Curia had been forced into a state of non-collaboration; with Pope John its failure to collaborate as the latter had hoped was its own, so that the Pope was left in what the Cardinal Lercaro has called the "institutional solitude" of Pope John.

All the same, his pontificate was not wholly lacking in measures directed towards the reform of the Curia. In 1958, a "rescritto di udienza" (rescript of audience) of John XXIII fixed an age limit of seventy-five years for departmental secretaries, although in some cases this remained a dead letter. At the beginning of 1960 he made known to the Roman cardinals that he did not wish any cardinal to hold more than one important office. Following this criterion, he proceeded to make a large number of nominations and changes among the office holders. Furthermore, he commanded the resident cardinals to attend the meetings of the congregations to which they belonged, provided they were in Rome at the time. Although these directives aimed at creating new customs, they were only applied to a few individual cases. In 1960 an investigation was made by the "American Institute of Management," which reassured anyone who might be feeling anxious (with that optimism so characteristic of "Readers Digest") that everything was well and (better still) that the Roman Curia held the first place among efficient public administrations. The three hundred people who made up the organisation (cardinals, secretaries, prelates, and employees) were doing an excellent job, as they had always done. A few men, laden with years and with offices, were successfully facing up to the enormous number of problems which had arisen in every part of the world. But the Catholic Church, which does not measure its organisations with the yardstick of an industrial manufacturing company, proved itself to be far more exacting than the flattering inquirers from beyond the ocean.

II / Requirements of Vatican Council II

The need to reform the central administration reached a point during Vatican II when it could no longer be repressed. The Council, by exploring once again the mystery of the Church, by its revived doctrine of the episcopate, and also by virtue of the mere fact that for more than four years bishops from all parts of the world were together in Rome, overthrew the pyramidcal and simply juridical conceptions of the Church, interpreted its "Romanity" simply as the source of its ecumenical character, freed it from political and cultural identification with the Mediterranean basin, and recognised the Pope as vested with the authority of the united episcopate. In this way it balanced the dogmatic affirmations of Vatican I.

1. THE NEED TO MAKE THE CURIA REALLY REPRESENTATIVE OF THE WHOLE WORLD

The first requirement which emerged from the Council was the need to make the Roman Curia universal. This required action on several planes. At the most elementary level, it required the dissociation of the central government machinery from its Italian context which, although it had gained great merit as a result of its collaboration with and protection of the Holy See, seemed by now like a limitation which was quite incompatible with the universal mission of the Catholic Church; this was the more obvious and urgent since at the same time the Italian Church itself was trying to escape from its dangerous confusion with the Roman Curia, and was beginning to assume its own autonomous juridical form. Neither young priests nor the laymen could easily understand why the Church—which by its very constitution is a supernational organism, catholic and ecumenical in character—should have a central government and a diplomatic corps in which there was such a marked predominance of the citizens of one particular nation.

The facts, however, showed that, if internationalisation were understood simply as an increase in the number of "foreigners" in the Curia, this would not have resolved the problem of making the Curia universal. Cardinals from countries other than Italy already stood at the head of some departments; some organisms of the Curia (as for example the Secretariat of State) had a markedly international character; among the consultors of every congregation were to be found representatives of different nations. But in most of these cases, the offices were not filled by people particularly likely to give a reforming impulse to the Roman Curia. They were much more like products of the "system" which had co-opted them than representatives at the centre of the Church of the ecclesiastical, theological, and pastoral needs of individual Churches and of catholic pluralism. It was, therefore, clear that a simply mechanical application of the international criterion would have been useless and even harmful, if there was not at the same time an authentic dialogue between the universal Church and the local Churches within the framework of the existing central government apparatus. This led to the conclusion that the reform of the Curia would have to be based on a new relationship between the episcopate and the governmental organs of the universal Church; because it remained true (as Cardinal Montini had indicated before the Council was opened) that catholics "listened with joy and veneration to the word of Rome, received norms and instructions, obeyed willingly, but often had the impression that there was no free and easy dialogue nor any invitation to collaborate, and that the unity of the Church was to be experienced in passive submission rather than in all the fun and joy of brotherhood which of course consisted in recognizing the Pope as our common father and as the centre of our family unity." Decisions taken by bishops were not seldom annulled by the Vatican without ever getting in touch with the bishops concerned; bishops were often forced to spend long hours in the waiting rooms of the various departments of 'the Curia, and then treated in a domineering manner by even the meanest Roman functionaries. These were some of the occurrences which prompted the conciliar criticisms of the Curia; they were not by any means the most scandalous ones. It was surely inevitable, therefore, that, once the powers of the episcopate had been defined in relation to the Universal Church, the Council should also lay down that "the Roman Pontiff, in carrying out his supreme, full, and immediate authority over the whole Church, avails himself of the various departments of the Roman Curia, which accordingly discharge their functions in his authority and in his name, *for the benefit of all the Churches and as a service to all the Holy Pastors";* and that it should resolve that a certain number of diocesan bishops should be added to the Roman departments so that they might present the Pope with "the thinking, the desires, and the needs of all Churches" (Decree "Christus Domnus", Nos. 9 and 10). It was, in fact, imperative that the pastoral spirit should be infused into a Curia which had become too closely attached to a juridical immobility of a peculiarly Roman brand, such as even the proposed reform of the Code of Canon Law was intending to abandon.

2. THE NEED TO DEFINE THE EXECUTIVE ROLE OF THE CURIA

The second major requirement was to find a better definition of the functions of a Curia which in principle could not be anything more than an executive organ, an instrument, an administration. In opposition to this principle, ever since the directive functions and the collegial powers of decision of the Consistory had begun to decline in the fifteenth century, the Curia had absorbed some ambiguous functions which were partly deliberative and partly executive, and had arrogated to itself the powers of decision in the shadow of the one and only authority to whom they rightly belonged, namely the Supreme Pontiff. Many members of the Curia regarded their own decisions exactly as if they were decisions made by the Pope. The second Vatican Council, in the course of many hours of dramatic debate, was forced to contest this claim. But it was also necessary (leaving aside particular cases) to define with great clarity the borderline between the Pope's own authority and the acts of the Roman Curia; to make clear just where legitimate execution of a superior order ended and where individual officers began to take unwarranted initiatives. For this reason it seemed a good idea to

56

return to the stage of collective direction and coordination which in older times was represented by consistorial meetings. Even if this did not completely recover a collegiate government at the summit of the Church, it would at least have remedied the muddle in the actual work, the confusion between spheres of responsibility, and the conflicts of authority between departments which used to occur. The need was felt for combining spheres of responsibility and for simplifying procedure. It was absurd that the intellectual training of future priests should be in the hands of three departments, viz., the Congregations of "Seminaries and Universities," of "Religious," and of "Propagation of the Faith."

3. THE NEED FOR ORGANIC RELATIONS BETWEEN THE "OLD" AND THE "NEW" CURIA

The third major need was to create an organic relationship on a basis of equality between the "old curia" and the "new curia." The latter consisted of three Secretariats (i) for Promoting Christian Unity, (ii) for Non-Christians, (iii) and for Non-Believers, as well as the *Consilium de laicis* and the Commission *"Justitia et Pax."* Even though Paul VI had expressed his opinions without any ambiguity (his *"Motu Proprio"* entitled "Finis Concilio" published on the 3 January 1966 had even "institutionalised" the Secretariat for Christian Unity), there remained real doubts as to whether these new institutions were in fact organs of the central government of the Church or not. Notwithstanding the Pope's efforts to ensure stability and co-responsibility between the old and the new curia, there were still very clear and serious risks of several bodies working along parallel lines.

4. THE NEED FOR IMPLEMENTING THE EVANGELICAL PRINCIPLE OF "SERVICE" WITHIN THE CURIA

Finally, there remained the need for translating the evangelical principle of "service" which the Council had rediscovered into a concrete reality by making precise juridical arrangements. In practical terms this meant abolishing the principle that the holders of major offices in the Curia could not be removed or transferred, and also the subdivision of responsibilities so as to counteract the tendency towards concentrating a large number of offices in the hands of a very few people. Some examples of this phenomenon may be given here. Cardinal Ottaviani (born 1890), apart from being a deputy prefect of the former Holy Office, was also a member of six other congregations and one tribunal. Cardinal Confalonieri (born 1893), a Deputy Prefect of the Consistory and a member of eight congregations for the Eastern Church, was also a member of six other congregations and one tribunal apart from being Vice-President of two financial bodies. Cardinal Amleto Cicognani (born 1883) was Secretary of State, Prefect of the Congregation for Extraordinary Ecclesiastical Affairs, and also a member of seven other congregations, President of two financial bodies and of the Commission for the Vatican City State.

This concentration of executive power in the hands of an "oligarchy" could be justified only in a small degree by the need for channelling the experience and competence of the various departments into the decisions of every single congregation. In reality the system of horizontal interchange at the level of heads of departments proved a severe brake on action; but its worst defect was represented by the "power groups," the obscure alliances which were formed behind the curtain of official secrecy which masked all Curial proceedings. It was also obvious that there was a great need to step the automatic mechanisms of promotion, which had led to the choice of people to fill offices at the nerve centers of the Curia being made by purely bureaucratic methods. This was true right up to the highest offices, which would eventually be crowned with a cardinal's hat. Some system of objective selection, possibly even by competitive examination, was needed to ensure that the best minds from every part of the world could make their contribution to the work of the Roman Curia, and to eliminate the possibilities of "patronage" so clearly implied by the system of co-option to the Curia.

1. THE SPEECH MADE BY PAUL VI

III / Preparation of the Reform

The speech with which Paul VI announced the reform of the Curia within three months of his election, was a masterpiece of delicacy and balanced argument. He succeeded in placing his finger on the worst defects of the Curia while at the same time giving it praise. He intimated to the members of the Curia what "had to be" without offending them; and, finally, he entrusted the Curia with the task of reforming itself, inviting its members to accept the Council and not to do anything that was not in line with the "will, judgment, or feeling" of the Pope.

His speech made a notable impression on the Curia. It influenced the second session of the Council, which had to deal with changing the structures of the Church and bringing them up to date. For a long time afterwards, both theologians and observers were discussing the significance of the new outlook and perspectives opened up by the Pope as regards placing representatives of the episcopate at the side of the "supreme head of the Church for the study and responsibility of ecclesiastical government." On the 30 November 1963 Paul VI published his Motu Proprio entitled "Pastorale munus," with which he conferred upon the bishops forty faculties and privileges which had up to then been the exclusive prerogative of Rome.

2. THE COMMISSION OF CARDINALS

It was known that the Pope had set up a commission for the reform of the Curia. Its chairman was Cardinal Francesco Roberti, (born at Pergola in 1889) who was Prefect of the Supreme Tribunal of the Apostolic Signature. An eminent expert on canon law, he was also the author of an interesting critical study of the chaotic state of affairs within the Curia prior to Pius. A prelate of the Sacred Roman Rota, Mons. Giovanni Pinna, was the commission's secretary. The choice had fallen upon men who belonged to the judiciary sector of the Curia and who therefore had a theoretical margin of independence with regard to the administrative sector. The same principle had been followed in the choice of members. Cardinal Andrea Jullien (born near Lyons in 1882), a jurist, was one of the few members of the Supreme Tribunal of the Apostolic Signature who did not hold offices of high responsibility in the curial congregations. Likewise, Cardinal Gioacchino Anselmo Albareda (a Benedictine monk, born at Barcelona in 1892), was not a member of the oligarchy of the Curia. When Cardinal Jullien died in 1964, his place on the commission was filled by Cardinal William Heard (born in Edinburgh in 1884) who was also a member of the Apostolic Signature. Cardinal Albareda (who died in 1966) was replaced by the seventy-seven year old Milanese Cardinal Efrem Forni, a diplomat and member of various congregations.

3. THE CONFLICT IN THE PREPARATORY STAGES

Contrary to the hopes which Paul VI had nurtured, the

staff did not succeed in emulating the rapidity with which the reform undertaken by Pius X had been prepared. Almost four years passed before the new reform saw the light of day.

The first phase of the work was spent in collecting the basic elements and above all in analysing the proposals put forward by the bishops during the preparatory phases of the Council and during the course of its actual sessions. The Roman Congregations were consulted, as were also bishops from every part of the world and the Rectors of the ecclesiastical colleges in Rome.

The task of drafting the text of a brief summary was undertaken during the second phase. Paul VI ordered a new consultation and gave further directives. The first of the thirteen drafts, through which this tormented preparation of the reform was subsequently to pass, was thus drawn up.

A continuous conflict between, on the one hand, a simple juridical face-lift of the Roman Curia and, on the other, the kind of "bringing-up-to-date" desired by the Council (which might have permeated the curial structures with the collegial and pastoral spirit of Vatican II) delayed its birth. It was clear then that the reform of a machine like the Curia called for the presence of one man who had the right to turn it inside out. Antoine de Saint Exupéry observed that "in an administration designed to obviate the drawbacks stemming from human caprice, the interlocking wheels are such as to repel the intervention of man. They do not desire the services of a watchmaker." This gives the measure of the audacity shown by Paul VI when he charged the Roman Curia with its own reform. It also helps to explain why he felt it necessary to take the reins of the reform into his own hands, in anticipation of the Synod of Bishops which is due to assemble quite soon.

The commission was disposed to make a series of decrees of only partial reform for each single congregation, a gradual process over a fairly long period of time. On this basis, the reform of the Holy Office was published at the end of the fourth session of the Council. The possibility of drafting a single comprehensive document rather than a lot of partial ones began to emerge only much later. As late as 23 December 1966, Paul VI, in an address to the cardinals, seemed still to be referring to the earlier concept when he announced that "some decrees" of reform were already ready, and that he hoped to be able to publish them "before long."

4. THE FINAL INTERVENTION BY PAUL VI

But the decrees which were "ready" not only needed to be coordinated in a clear vision of the whole. They were also in need of a new inspiration. And this in turn called for a "new work." Mons. Pinna, the commission's secretary, said much later, when he was trying to recount the many vicissitudes in drafting, that "this new work was followed and personally directed throughout the final phase by the Holy Father himself, who did us the honour of taking the chair himself at the study meetings which were also attended by two highly placed prelates in the Secretariat of State, Mons. Angelo dell'Acqua and Mons. Jaques Martin, in addition to the commission's secretary. The Supreme Pontiff in this manner perfected the text of the document, discussing and weighing with great care every single expression and paying the greatest attention to the new observations and desires, which (at the invitation of the Holy Father himself) had been expressed by the heads of the curial congregations after they had examined those parts of the draft schemes which directly concerned them."[3] This meant that the Commission of cardinals had to all intents and purposes been dismissed; in fact, only its secretary now remained. It also meant that the Pope had ordered a new consultation and that it was, therefore, the case of an entirely "new" work rather than the "third phase" of a work begun in 1963.

IV / The Line
Followed by Paul VI

During the spring of 1966, Paul VI began to put into effect a plan for converting the Roman Curia from the inside without further delay. In his speech to the cardinals, just before Christmas 1965, he had already clearly revealed his intentions. "New labours, new responsibilities, a new formulation, a new organisation,—all these, no matter how much we sincerely try to simplify matters, will certainly mean further additions and complications, and still more responsibilities. We are certain that the Roman Curia, which is now more open and more expert as the result of the experiences of the ecumenical council, will know how to face the problems of the post-conciliar period in the proper manner; and this not only by virtue of its new efficiency on the administrative and professional plane, but also on account of its high level of probity and intelligence, which lead it to cultivate and practice the virtues inherent in its mission with even greater fervour than before."

---

3. cf. L'Osservatore Romano, 19th August 1967

1. ARCHBISHOP GARRONE AND CANON MOELLER

Gabriel Garrone, the Archbishop of Toulouse, was appointed Deputy Prefect of the Sacred Congregation of Seminaries and Universities on the 3 February 1966. Cardinal Giuseppe Pizzardo, one of the most influential members of the curial oligarchy, still kept the office of Prefect, which he had held since the times of Pius XII, notwithstanding his eighty-nine years of age. But at his side there was now a sixty-five year old "pastor," invested with full powers, who had been the vice-chairman of the conference of the French Episcopate, the very man who during the Council's meeting on the 17th November 1964 had called for the reform of the Congregation of Seminaries.

A Belgian, Canon Charles Moeller, was appointed Under-Secretary of the Sacred Congregation for the Teaching of the Faith on the 12th February 1966.

On the 23 April 1966, in the presence of the Curia all lined up on the faldstools of St. John Lateran to celebrate the jubilee of the Council in Rome, Paul VI spoke as follows: "Do not let us use the true faith which has been given us for our benefit and enjoyment as a basis either for pride or for privilege, as a pretext for vain polemics or for offences against charity, or as an excuse for the egotistical laziness so often characteristic of the well-off; let us rather make it a stimulus to greater study, to more fervent prayer, to mutual understanding, and to greater zeal. Whatever we may have thought about the various opinions of the Council before it promulgated its conclusions, to-day we have to respect and obey the conciliar decisions with complete sincerity and without reserve; we have to be eager and ready to give them our allegiance in thought, in action, and in conduct. The Council has been a great innovation; not everyone was disposed to understand and appreciate it. But we must now attribute the conciliar doctrines to the magisterium of the Church, or rather to the inspiration of the Holy Spirit; and we must accept the texts of the teachings and the precepts which the Council transmits to the Church with unwavering, unanimous faith. In this, too, let us find a welcome stimulus for ourselves and set a good example to our neighbours, since it is our duty to interpret this teaching and to encourage acceptance of it."

Before he ever took in hand any technical modifications of the Church's structures, Paul VI was calling for a change in heart and mind of the central administration of the Church.

Cardinal Ciriaci died on the 30 December 1966, at the age

of eighty-three years, and thus left vacant the office of Prefect of the Sacred Congregation of the Council, which had been created by Pius IV in 1564 to enforce observance of the disciplinary decisions of the Council of Trent, and which had later been entrusted with the whole discipline of the clergy and the faithful. Ten days later, the chairmanship of the *Consilium de laicis* and the Commission *"Justitia et Pax"* was entrusted to a diocesan bishop, Cardinal Roy of Quebec. Jurisdiction over the "Christian Community," traditionally held by the Congregation of the Council, was transferred to the Consilium. On the 23 February 1967 Paul VI made a further move within his overall strategy. The secretaryship of the Synod of Bishops was given to a Polish bishop, Mgr. Ladislao Rubin, while the former secretary of the Council, Archbishop Felici, was appointed Deputy Prefect of the Commission for the reform of the Code of Canon Law.

2. CARDINAL VILLOT AND BISHOP SCHROEFFER

During this time certain conservative organs of the Italian press were carrying on a campaign, more of calumny than of serious opposition, against "the French soviet" in the Roman Curia. To this end they published certain information and more forecasts whose very accuracy showed beyond any doubt that they were inspired by certain circles inside the Vatican itself.

Paul VI remained unperturbed. On the 8 April 1967 he took yet another step forward in his plans for reform. He called another French diocesan bishop, Cardinal Jean Villot of Lyons (born in 1905) to be head of the Congregation of the Council. At the same time, he transferred Mgr. Staffa to the Apostolic Signature, placing him as Deputy Prefect to Cardinal Roberti, and pointed to Cardinal Cento (who at the age of eighty-four years had renounced his position as head of the Sacred Apostolic Penitentiary and had thus become the first of the curial cardinals to resign) as an example which others among the more elderly cardinals of the Curia might well follow. Cardinal Aloisi Masella, eighty-eight years old, Prefect of the Sacred Congregation of the Sacraments, also was given a Deputy Prefect to assist him, in the person of Mgr. Francesco Carpino, who had gained a reputation in the Sicilian diocese of Monreale as a "moderate," and who had then been called to the Curia, to the Sacred Consistorial Congregation. It was obvious that the Pope's idea in creating Deputy Prefects was to devise a means of transferring the effective power of directing the congregations, offices, and tribunals from the curial cardinals who were now too advanced in years to men who were much younger.

On the 17 May 1967 Paul VI gave the post that Mgr. Staffa had held for six years to a German, Mgr. Josef Schroeffer (born 1903), who was bishop of the three hundred and fifty thousand catholics in Eichstat, the smallest diocese in Germany. Mgr. Schroeffer had obtained the largest number of votes at the elections to the conciliar commissions in 1962.

3. THE CONSISTORY OF 1967

The creation of new cardinals in June 1967 enabled Paul VI to unblock other situations with a view to the reform of the Curia. Among the new cardinals were to be found the Secretary of the Congregation for Extraordinary Ecclesiastical Affairs (Archbishop Samoré), the Substitute of the Secretariat of State (Archbishop dell'Acqua), and the Secretary of the Congregation for the Teaching of the Faith (Mgr. Parente). The Secretary of the Congregation for the Propagation of the Faith (Archbishop Sigismondi), who had been one of the most likely candidates for a cardinal's hat, had died at the end of May. A number of offices of crucial importance thus fell vacant, to be filled by the Pope as he chose. The Consistory also brought back to Rome some nuncios who (by the standards of the Curia) were still young: for example, the Apostolic Delegate in the United States, Mgr. Vagnozzi (1906), and the nuncio in Portugal, Maximilian de Furstenberg (1904).

The Consistory reinforced the authority of Mgr. Garrone as the head of the Congregation of Seminaries, and made it possible immediately to appoint a successor to Cardinal Ruffini, who had died on the 11 June 1967. The new Archbishop of Palermo is Cardinal Carpino.

Paul VI balanced the influx of "new men" by interchanging prelates from one office to another. Mgr. Civardi was appointed Secretary of the Consistorial Congregation, thereby crowning a career of thirty years. Mgr. Agostino Casaroli, the Vatican's ambassador for difficult missions in Eastern Europe, succeeded the newly created Cardinal Samoré as Secretary of the Vatican's "Foreign Office." The French Dominican Father Mgr. Paul Philippe, moved to the Secretaryship of the Congregation of the Teaching of the Faith, where he replaced Mgr. Parente, who was now a cardinal. An old friend of the pope, Mgr. Mauro, who had been Chief of Protocol, assumed the Secretaryship of the Congregation of Religious. Similarly, the appointment of Mgr. Loris Capovilla, who had been private secretary to Pope John to be archbishop of Chieti, could be plausibly explained as a prelude to "purging the Papal household."

4. TRUSTED COLLABORATORS

The arrival of other "new men" (this time Italians) enabled Paul VI to feel satisfied that he had now formed a team of collaborators whom he could trust, so far as the difficult circumstances within which he always has to work will allow. He recalled the Apostolic Delegate, Mgr. Giovanni Benelli (1921), from Africa and appointed him Substitute in the Secretariat of State. He also called to Rome Mgr. Sergio Pignedoli (1910), Apostolic Delegate in Canada, and entrusted him with the Secretaryship of the Congregation for the Propagation of the Faith, which is headed by Cardinal Agagianian. The two new men had a number of things in common: their relative youth, their long-standing friendship with the Pope, and their diplomatic experience which they had gained outside the old-style political forms and more in line with an evangelical conception of the mission of the Catholic Church.

1. THE MOTU PROPRIO "PRO COMPERTO SANE"

V / Answers Given by the Reform

Each of the principal requirements formulated by the Council has now been met, clearly and precisely (though not always exhaustively) in the documents which are destined to turn the sixteenth-century Curia into the Curia of Vatican II.

To the primary need to make the Curial machinery really co-extensive with the whole world, Paul VI has replied with his *Motu Proprio* "Pro comperto sane" which was actually published on the 12 August 1967, although it is dated six days earlier. He laid down that a number of diocesan bishops (usually seven) should become full members of each Congregation. "Today more than ever before," as is emphasized in the document, "the problems of the Church have become world-wide; if they are to be solved effectively, we need an attitude of mind open to argument and new perception and a practical experience which is authentically catholic." The purpose of introducing diocesan bishops into the Curial Congregations as "members with full rights" was to make the Curia capable of "efficiently discharging the new and heavy responsibilities which are the logical result of the decisions and the votes of the ecumenical Council." The papal decision meant that responsibility for decisions in the Roman Curia was no longer the exclusive prerogative of the cardinals, who had hitherto been the only people fully and unquestionably entitled to sit around the tables of the Congregations. The participation of the resident bishops, who still hold full responsibility for their sees, will bring the problems of the pastoral life of the Church in all continents right into the administrative Curia. A new, stable, and personal link between the centre and the circumference, between the central government and the episcopal conferences, will thus take the place of the bureaucratic relations and intermittent exchanges of former times, in which travel and communications were difficult. The "pastors" who were already members of the Curia, are now re-inforced by an influx of contemporary and continuous experience, of men who have reached maturity, at the nerve-centre of our rapidly evolving history; and the benefits were no less great out on the circumference, where the local bishops could now obtain from direct collaboration in the central government of the Church a world-wide vision of her problems and an increased sensitivity to the exigencies of catholic unity.

These were the promises implicit in the decision with which Paul VI gave effect to one of the wishes expressed by the Council Fathers. It only remains to ask whether the membership of diocesan bishops may not become just as "symbolic" as that of cardinals who are also diocesan bishops residing in their sees and who, although they were full members of the various congregations, could attend their meetings only on very rare occasions. A very careful analysis of the *Motu Proprio* is therefore imperative.

The document lays down that the diocesan bishops should attend only the plenary sessions of the congregations, which will be held once a year only, to discuss the most important matters (unless special circumstances intervene). The Pope is here concerned to avoid "the difficulties which could be caused in diocesan sees by the frequent and prolonged absences of their bishops." The other (non-plenary) meetings would continue "according to established custom," with just the cardinals and those bishops who found themselves in Rome attending.

It is therefore clear that the real effectiveness of the bishops' membership will depend on the "matters of greatest importance" on which they would be consulted, and also on the length of the annual plenary meetings, which could easily be turned into sessions of purely formal character where carefully pre-fabricated solutions were ratified and re-inforced by episcopal blessing. It will depend, above all, on the representative nature of the bishops chosen to attend these sessions. The Motu Proprio proposed a method of selection the very complexity of which made it possible to guess how great was the effort that had been made to find a compromise between two different views. On the one hand, the Curia would have liked to nominate the bishops itself; on the other hand, the episcopal conferences in each country insisted on being responsible for nominating the participants, so that the bishops to be sent to Rome would be truly in a position to "represent the thinking, the desires and the necessities of all the Churches before the Supreme Pontiff," as had been laid down in the Conciliar decree. The procedure proposed in the Motu Proprio gives the Cardinal Prefect of each Congregation the initiative of "making suitable researches and enquiries within the episcopal conferences and, if this seemed necessary, obtaining a list of episcopal candidates." It also gives him the initiative of proposing to the Pope the names of those whom he would have "freely" chosen. Evidently, we are here dealing with a form of co-option by the Curia rather than with nomination by the local episcopate.

2. THE APOSTOLIC CONSTITUTION "REGIMINI ECCLESIAE UNIVERSAE"

The desire to have a Curia a little less Roman and more universal is expressed with even greater force in the Apostolic Constitution "Regimini Ecclesiae Universae" which the Pope signed on the 15 August 1967 and published three days later. This document puts together the ideas for a comprehensive structure of the new Curia into one overall perspective.

The inclusion of elements "from every continent" in the central administration, the insistence on "pastoral experience" as an essential qualification of the new "officials," the obligation to keep in communication with the episcopal conferences of every country, the rapid and respectful service which the Curia would have to give to diocesan bishops: all these were norms directed to this end. All the same, some of the detailed provisions seemed to be rather lagging behind the directives (some of them imperative) which the Council had given, and were not even so far-reaching as the coherent norms contained in the *Motu Proprio* "Ecclesiae Sanctae" which Paul VI had issued on the 6 August 1966 for the purpose of implementing these directives.

a) *The case of the "episcopal direction" of "Propaganda Fide"*

The most serious case appeared to be the one concerning the reform of "Propaganda Fide."

In 1966, the *Motu Proprio* "Ecclesiae Sanctae" had provided that twenty-four representatives should participate with full voting rights in the direction of this department. These were to consist of twelve prelates from the missions, four representatives from the other regions, four superiors-general of Religious Orders or Societies, and four representatives of the Pontifical Organizations. There were to be two meetings per annum. The names of the candidates were to be submitted directly to the Pope by the episcopal conferences, the religious orders, and the pontifical associations, and the Pope was to choose the representatives from among these candidates.

A year later, the *Motu Proprio* "Pro Comperto Sane" re-affirmed these provisions, which had not yet been put into practice.

The *Motu Proprio* was greatly weakened, however, when the Apostolic Constitution was published only seven days later on the 15 August. This said that "both bishops from the missions nominated by the Roman Pontiff, and representatives of the superiors of the religious orders and the Pontifical Organizations shall have the right to attend all plenary sessions of the Congregation as full members, and with voting powers if it shall so please the said Pontiff. As regards the number of such members, reference is made to the *Motu Proprio* 'Ecclesiae Sanctae' of the 6 August 1966 and to a specific instruction which is to be issued by the Congregation."

A comparison of the various texts makes it obvious that the missionary bishops are no longer to participate in the "direction" but only in the "plenary congregations" of Propaganda Fide. They are no longer always and exclusively to have a full, effective vote, but merely "also" an effective vote "if it shall so please the Pontiff." There is no longer any reference to candidates being nominated by the episcopal conferences, but only to nomination from above. It remains doubtful whether the bishops are to be called to meetings twice a year, or only once, as the latest norms suggest.

It is well known that the directors of "Progaganda Fide" are strongly opposed to the reform. The department had not even succeeded in changing its name, but had simply added a new name to the old one. In this manner it had become the congregation with the longest name of all, in which past and future were freely mixed. "*Sacra congregatio pro gentium evangelizatione seu de Propaganda Fide*" was to be its new name.

b) *The "reform" of the Congregation of Religious*

Similarly as regards the reform of the Congregation of Religious, no trace is to be found of the papal provision of the 6 August 1966 by which the Unions of Superiors-General, both for men and women, were to be heard and consulted by means of a council to be set up within the congregation. The Constitution of the 15th August 1967 limited itself to saying that the Congregation of Religious "will take care to use the work of the Superiors-General in the most suitable manner." The Motu Proprio "Pro Comperto Sane" had laid down that ten diocesan bishops should be admitted as members to the plenary assemblies of the department, not merely seven, and that three of them would have to be chosen from a list of candidates prepared by the Roman Union of Superiors-General. Moreover, although there was a strong current of opinion in favour of transferring authority over the secular institutes to the *Consilium de laicis,* the reform of the Curia now confirms their unnatural dependence on the Congregation of Religious, which is now renamed *"sacra congregatio pro religiosis et institutis saecularibus."*

c) *A homogeneous model of episcopal "participation"*

In much the same way, the reform has not accepted the proposal of the post-consiliar commission for the institution of a "Superior Council" within the Department for Catholic Teaching, which is the new name of the Congregation of Seminaries and Universities. In this case, however, the proposal had not previously received the blessing of a pontifical Motu Proprio. It only remains to explain why, contrary to the expectations of Cardinal Garrone himself, the reform has not united within this congregation all authority which is currently shared with "Propaganda Fide" and the Congregation of Religious.

On the whole, one gets the impression that it has been thought best to reduce the participation of the bishops (or of religious) in the curial congregations to one single model in order to satisfy the need for the structures. All the same, this model marks a retreat from some of the points captured by the Council: — for example, the one which had brought the bishops directly to assume full powers in the direction of "Propaganda Fide" as a forward-looking application of the principles of episcopal collegiality.

3. PAPAL SECRETARIAT AND "COUNCIL OF MINISTERS"

The immaturity from which the doctrine of the collegiate authority of the bishops within the universal Church continues to suffer, has clearly been the decisive factor in setting limits to the reform of the Curia.

The document issued by Paul VI meets the need for reducing the central machinery of government to purely executive functions quite satisfactorily; but it does not seem to accept the proposal for reconstituting in an up-to-date form the Consistory of cardinals "co-responsible" for central government as practised in earlier ages. One general norm has been affirmed, namely the equality in status of all congregations. This was reinforced by the Pope's decision to give up the Prefecture of both the Congregation for the Teaching of the Faith and Consistorial Congregation. This latter Congregation is now renamed "pro ecclesiis orientalibus." Further, the Constitution lays down in a forcible manner the principle that every decision of any department is subject to the Pope's approval and that no matter of importance may be dealt with except with his knowledge. The reform underpins these principles with new and better organizations including a completely reconstructed Secretariat of State and a newly created body to coordinate all the other departments: this is the Council of Cardinal Prefects, to be convened by the Secretary of State as and when required.

The reform of the Secretariat of State entails the abolition of all purely political concerns. On the one hand, the department for "ordinary affairs" (with its "Substitute" who was particularly concerned with Italy) has been suppressed; on the other hand the department for extraordinary affairs has been absorbed (together with the Congregation for Extraordinary Ecclesiatical Affairs) in a kind of "Foreign Office," the "consilium pro publicis Ecclesiae negotiis." This re-organization has considerable advantages. The Pope will now have a better "image" as essentially a religious personage; Italian affairs are now merged in the general problem of the Church's relations with States in all parts of the world. The link between the two organisms lies in the person of the Secretary of State, the only cardinal who will now be allowed to hold two offices in the Curia. It seems to offer sufficient guarantees as regards the clarity of the relations between the authority of the Pope and that of the congregations, as the Secretariat of State is charged with the institutional task of assisting the Pope "in the care of all the Church and in the relations with the departments of the Roman Curia." The functions of the "Consilium pro publicis Ecclesiae negotiis," on the other hand, are defined as "dealing with matters relating to relationships with civil governments."

In spite of this clear frontier between the religious sphere and the political sphere, the reform has not yet sanctioned another requirement which had long been germinating in the "People of God" and finally came to conscious fruition; indeed, after Vatican II, it seemed thoroughly legitimate. This was to do away with a title which has so secular and political a flavour as "Secretariat of State," an anachronistic hangover from the times when the Popes were also temporal sovereigns. The Apostolic Constitution has rather timidly added the title "Papal Secretariat" to the old name; this might have been greeted as a sign of an authentically conciliar character, had it not been found in unnatural company and surrounded by impossible compromises.

The other instrument which helps to throw into relief the purely executive function of the Curia, is the "Council of the Cardinal Prefects." Many people have compared this organism to a "Council of Ministers," such as is usually provided for in the constitutions of modern States. Even Mons. Pinna, in the course of the press conference on the Apostolic Constitution, when reading the text which was subsequently to appear in the "Osservatore Romano" as an authentic interpretation of the law, seemed to have given this comparison some official standing when he affirmed that "it will be a great help in co-ordinating the work of the departments of the Curia if from time to time the cardinal prefects meet with the Secretary of State, somewhat on the lines of a Council of Ministers in the various modern States." Mons. Pinna went even further than this, and suggested to those who were trying to get a better idea of the nature of this "Council" that they should read an article published that same day in an Italian catholic newspaper.[4] The article in question had again argued the need to revive the old collegiate functions of the Consistory of cardinals with the Roman Pontiff. All this quite naturally led to the "council of ministers" being interpreted in a collegiate sense. But this interpretation was a good way away from the functions which the Apostolic Constitution had really attributed to it. The document, in fact, did not go beyond these words: "The Cardinal Secretary of State may, whenever he deems it opportune, convene the cardinal prefects in order to co-ordinate everybody's work, to impart any news, and to receive advice."

The purpose of the "Council of Ministers" is thus substantially of a "functional" nature as regards co-ordinating the executive powers of the Roman Curia, and did not yet adumbrate the possibility of a collegiate elaboration of decisions in relation to the universal Church. We have here an instrument designed to ensure a kind of general direction of the work of the curial departments and to make sure that the lines of government laid down by the Pope were being faithfully followed. But even if the consultative

---

4. cf. L'Avvenire d'Italia, 18th August 1967

functions of the "council" may yet be strengthened, it is quite impossible to see how it could ever become a permanent extension of the Synod of Bishops unless there were to be an authentic acceptance and translation into practice of the conciliar principles of episcopal collegiality.

4. ORGANIC RELATIONS BETWEEN THE "OLD" AND THE "NEW" CURIA

The constitution published by Paul VI meets the need for organic relations between the "old curia" and the "new curia" by making the three secretariats for Promoting Christian Unity, for Non-Christians, and for Non-Believers, together with the Commission for Justice and Peace and the *Consilium de laicis,* integral parts of the organic plan of the Roman Curia on the basis of full parity with the other departments. The text still shows traces of resistance to this integration. At the beginning of the document it is stated that the Roman Curia "consist of Congregations, Tribunals, Offices, and Secretariats." Moreover, in the main body of the Constitution the regulations concerning the Secretariats, the *Consilium de laicis,* and the Commission *"Justitia et Pax,"* were placed immediately after those relating to the Papal Secretariat, the "Consilium pro publicis Ecclesiae negotiis," and the old Congregations now reformed, but before those relating to Tribunals and Offices. This was yet another indication of the great speed with which the document had been prepared. There is also the fact that the new bodies, which have come into being on the tide of Vatican II, have not only been placed on a footing of juridical parity with the "old curia" but have also been given the right to be represented within the old departments. This representation was no longer to be on an empirical or purely voluntary basis, but an objective and obligatory means of communication and co-responsibility. The chairmen of the three secretariats were to be full members of the Congregation for the Evangelisation of the People. The Congregation for the Eastern Churches is to have among its full members, not only the cardinals chosen by the Pope and the Eastern patriarchs *ex-officio,* but also the Chairman of the Secretariat for Promoting Christian Unity. Furthermore, the Congregation for Bishops was called upon to "work hand in glove with the department 'de laicis' in certain fields." As regards the relationship between the Congregation of Rites and the Council for Liturgical Reform, the Constitution lays down that the latter was to have competence over the revision of the liturgical texts and indeed even liturgical reforms in general, but adds that the Council's final conclusions are to be submitted to a plenary session of the Ritual Section of the Congregation. It is clear that the 'Council' could be dissolved as soon as it had discharged its institutional task of launching the conciliar reform of the liturgy; after that, all practical applications would then be controlled by the ancient Congregation of the Roman Curia.

5.   EVEN THE CURIA DIES

But the most ample and most couragous reform introduced by Paul VI in his Apostolic Constitution is the one with which he meets the need for translating the evangelical principle of "service" into fact. The Pope has finally abolished the traditional principle of the irremovability of office holders, and has brought the Curia within the scope of his scheme for preventing sclerosis which had been proposed at an earlier date to diocesan bishops when they were invited to offer their resignations on reaching the age of seventy-five. The terms of this extension are, in fact, more rigorous.

The document makes no reference to an age limit to be applied to members of the curia; this problem was deferred to a "general regulation" which has yet to be prepared. But a possibly harsher principle was introduced, and applied to the offices of greatest responsibility. Cardinal prefects, members of the departments (be they cardinals or bishops), secretaries and consultors "may not hold office for more than five years." The Pope was left free to dismiss or to confirm them in office at the end of the five-year period. At his death, however, all of them automatically cease to hold office, with the sole exception of the Substitute of the Papal Secretariat, who will be responsible to the Sacred College. The new Constitution, naturally, gives the new Pope the right to confirm office holders as he deems fit; but he cannot do so until three months after his election. Decisions of such importance cannot be taken immediately, while the new Pope is still submerged by the profusion of compliments showered upon him and while he is going through his "novitiate" (as Pope John described this period). This is also a time in which he will be drawing up his programme and taking stock of the situation for which he will be answerable to God and to men. In the past, a new Pope's programme always ran the risk of having to be tailored so as to suit the personal idiosyncrasies of the men then holding office in the Curia.

It is necessary to recall the difficulties of Pope John XXIII and Pope Paul VI, when they found themselves after their election without suitable men to put their programmes of government into effect. The reform carried out by Paul VI ensures that on the death of a Pope his successor will be left completely free to form the team which he considers the best for carrying out his programme.

73

The principle that all offices are to lapse automatically on the death of a Pope is bound to have an enormous influence, even as regards the internal reform of the Roman Curia. For the first time in its history, the "everlasting" idea which it had of itself has been given a real blow. The Curia now has to die every time that a Pope dies. This will finally undermine the sense of superiority and perpetual stability which for many centuries has turned the Pope into a king and the Curia into the effective government of the Catholic Church. Everything has once again become mortal, provisional and time-conditioned, no longer indispensable, and basically more human and more humble. The Church, and only the Church, holds within itself the promise of the permanence of Christ to the end of time. The Roman Curia has lost its supreme standing and now has to resign itself to simply rendering the Church a service for a fixed term.

The five-yearly rotation of offices has also created the possibility of a new flexibility which will allow the Pope, in a period of great and rapid changes, periodically to change the people in office to meet new and continuously altering circumstances. This has in turn made it possible to generate a new dynamism in curial work which has been quite unknown during the preceding period of bureaucratic security. "The purpose of the time limit imposed on membership of the Congregations or on the employment of secretaries," said Mons. Pinna, forgetting at the time that the new norms were also to apply to the prefects, "is to keep on bringing fresher forces and open minds to the delicate and difficult task of directing such important organisms." It seems possible that the principle of a time-limit to holding any office was applied to the cardinal prefects only at the last moment, and only as the result of the Pope's exceptionally strenuous efforts in that direction. The fact remains, however, that the new regulations regarding the five-year term and the automatic lapse of all offices at the death of a Pope, which have now been made public, have broken the automatic nature of the careers and given the supreme pontiff a liberty of action which he did not previously possess. The Apostolic Constitution further states quite explicitly that "anyone elected to particular office cannot thereby claim the right to move up to an even higher office." It is not difficult to hear in this phrase the echo of certain episodes which, although the great majority of the Curia are good, devout priests with no thought of self-interest, had actually taken place, some of them even during the pontificate of Paul VI. Last but not least, the regulation which prevents the accumulation of several offices in the hands of one man has eliminated for ever the danger of the growth of a new curial oligarchy.

74

6. THE NEW INSTITUTIONS

The decision to form a "Prefecture of the Economy," directed jointly by three cardinals one of whom would act as chairman, and having powers to co-ordinate and supervise the various Vatican administrations (including the autonomous ones) is also playing a significant part in the internal reform of the Roman Curia. Nothing has yet been laid down regarding the publication of annual statements of accounts relating to the Holy See; but everything leads one to suppose that it is Pope Paul's desire to restore clarity, unity, and control from above to this particular sector. One of the principal purposes in forming this new body is to avoid the suspicions and calumnies which have always been fostered by the excessive mystery surrounding Vatican finances, and to eliminate the temptation (which is always present, even if it is hidden) of lapsing into non-evangelical attitudes. In spite of some early statements ("it would seem to be very useful to call in laymen for consultation and advice whenever the subject in hand may require or suggest this"), no layman has in fact been given a leading position in this "Ministry of Vatican Accounts." The Constitution published by Paul VI has widened the field from which consultors may be recruited to cover every sector of the "people of God" in every part of the world, and therefore also to include "laymen distinguished for their virtue, knowledge, and experience." Much, however, still remains to be done before laymen will be able to take up posts in the Roman Curia which may not be ecclesial, but which are certainly "in temporalibus."

Many "dead branches" which the Vatican has inherited from the period of the Renaissance have been swept away. These include the Datary, the Sacred Congregation of Ceremonies, the Chancery of Briefs, the Secretariat of Briefs to Princes and the Secretariat of Latin Letters, the Stewardship, and the office of the "Maestro di Camera." New, more up-to-date organizations have been created; these include the Statistical Office and an administrative section in the Supreme Tribunal of the Apostolic Signature. This latter increased the legal safeguards and the possibilities of appeal for those who feel that they have suffered some injustice through some act of the Roman Curia. The old Vatican "court" is now replaced by a "prefecture of the Apostolic Palace" charged with the organization of public and private audiences, ceremonies, the Pope's pilgrimages, and the audiences granted to foreign Heads of State. The number of congregations has been reduced to nine (for the Teaching of the Faith, for the Eastern Churches, for Bishops, of the Sacraments, of

Rites, for the Clergy, of Religious and for Secular Institutes, for Catholic Teaching, for the evangelization of the people), and the Papal Secretariat and the Council for the Public Affairs of the Church were placed at their head. The picture is completed by the Secretariat for Christian Unity, the Secretariat for Non-Christians, the Secretariat for Non-Believers, the Consilium de laicis, and the Commission "Justitia et Pax." The judicial sector has been made even more independent; it now comprises the Supreme Tribunal of the Apostolic Signature, the Sacred Roman Rota, and the Sacred Apostolic Penitentiary. The administration offices have been simplified and modernized; these comprise the Apostolic Chancery, the Prefecture of the Economy of the Holy See, the Apostolic Camera (for the administration of material assets when the Holy See is vacant), the Administration of the property of the Holy See, the Prefecture of the Apostolic Palace, and the Statistical Institute. All these offices are placed under the direction of the Papal Secretariat, whose province is now enlarged to cover the Papal Commission for Means of Social Communication and the Press Office of the Holy See as well.

VI / Between Past and Future

Even now that it has been reformed, the Curia still presents a very complex organization in which both old and new are co-existing. Some of the principles of the reform could undoubtedly breathe new life and vigour into the old body; but a great deal still depends upon the spirit and the manner in which men will accept them. It is still too early to know whether the reform will succeed in transforming the Curia of the Council of Trent into the Curia of Vatican II.

The reading of this very long document — one hundred and thirty-six articles, occupying three full pages of the "Osservatore Romano," and published in Latin (notwithstanding the document's own recommendation that the principal modern languages should also be used) — left one with an impression not very different from the one suggested by the official commentator when he reminded the assembled journalists of the words Paul VI had used at the opening of the second session of the Council: "The reform at which the Council aims is not then a subversion of the present life of the Church, nor is it a rupture with its traditions inasmuch as these are essential and venerable, but rather a homage to these very traditions which one longs to liberate from all out-dated and defective forms in order to make them more genuine."

76

If one may use Saint Exupery's simile (quoted above), many of the wheels are new, but the watch remains the same. Perhaps one day it will become possible to see that its hands are in fact showing the right time, the hour of the universal Church; that there is at last an administration capable of resolving new problems, because it has abandoned the methods of the past; that the loftiest ideals have not fallen into the hands of the least suitable men; that the Roman Curia has been moved nearer to the Church of the Council, and nearer to the world of the twentieth century.

III.

SOME SOCIOLOGICAL OBSERVATIONS

A Social Organizational View

of the Catholic Church

Andrew M. Greeley

If there is one thing that is clear in contemporary writing about the Catholic Church, it is that it is a community and a people. Indeed, some of us have heard this so often in recent years, we're probably tired of hearing it. (But it ought to be noted that the communitarian mention of the Church is still stressed far more in theory than it is in practice.) Frequently, especially in amateur theologizing and sociologizing about the Church, one would gain the impression that the Church as a community is somehow opposed to the Church as a structure—as though the ideal would be to have a Christian community without structure. It rarely occurs to such commentators that a community without structure is a non-existent community, because all human groups, even the most simple, quickly evolve established patterns of behavior and agreed-upon norms to regulate these patterns of behavior. In other words, even the most simple community has structure and laws. Those who wish to eliminate laws and or-

Father Andrew M. Greeley is a secular priest of the Archdiocese of Chicago. He is presently a Senior Study Director at the National Opinion Research Center, University of Chicago. Father Greeley has published several books on the life of the Church from a sociologist's point of view. Among the more recent: THE CATHOLIC EXPERIENCE: AN INTERPRETATION OF THE HISTORY OF AMERICAN CATHOLICISM; THE CHANGING CATHOLIC COLLEGE; THE UNCERTAIN TRUMPET: THE CATHOLIC PRIESTHOOD IN MODERN AMERICA.

ganizationalism in the Church and replace them with affection and love, show little understanding of men or of society.

I have been assured on occasion that if the Church is a society like other human societies, it is not a sign of God's intervention in history and that, therefore, in order to be a sign of such divine intervention, the Church must be a society that cannot be compared to other human groups. Under such circumstances, of course, any attempt to evaluate the Church's activities from the point of view of the theory of social organization is bound to be frustrating. Those who do not agree with you, whether they be members of the new breed or the old breed, can simply shrug their shoulders and observe, "But the Church isn't a human society—it's something divine." The sociologist, under such circumstances, is forced to say, "For a society that isn't a human society, it surely behaves remarkably like one and has so behaved for over nineteen hundred years." The sociologist is also forced to remark that from the perspective of his theological innocence, to say that the Church cannot be divine if it is a human society is rather like saying that Christ could not be divine if He had a human nature. Indeed, the sociologist might even go so far as to say that the very humanness of the Church as a society might very well be both a stumbling block and folly (to use the Pauline terms) to modern sociological simplicists.

Frequently it has seemed to me that a kind of theological Hobbsianism can be observed in some commentaries on the contemporary Church. One has the impression from such writings that organization and administration are bad things—that they stunt human spontaneity and freedom, interfere with human love, and frustrate the growth of the human spirit. The social scientist is tempted to marvel at such a view of organization and administration, since it seems to imply that mankind has made no progress in the understanding of social organization since the death of John Hobbs; as both Aristotle and contemporary behavioral scientists realize, administration, organization, and even regulation exist to promote the freedom of the human spirit, not prohibit it, and several scholarly disciplines, as well as a vast amount of existing empirical research, suggest how the Iron Law of Oligarchy (according to which organizations always frustrate the ends for which they were brought into being) can be inhibited. If the Church is not a human organization, then the scholarship of the behavioral sciences can be ignored. But if it is, it would be singularly inappropriate for Catholicism not to pay some attention, at least, to what social organizational research might have to say about its internal renewal.

Assuming, therefore, that at least some kind of analogical comparison of the Church to other human organizations is still theologically valid, it is my intention to contend that the problem with the Church is not, as Ivan Illich has suggested, that it has too much organization, but rather that it does not have good enough organization, and in many instances, that it simply does not have enough organization. I would go far as to argue that in many respects the progress of renewal within Roman Catholicism will not be successful unless new and more efficient organization is generated; the appearance of both the Episcopal Synod and the National Hierarchies suggest that this is precisely what is going on. Furthermore, I would contend that supernaturalists like Monsignor Illich to the contrary notwithstanding, these new organizations are much more likely to facilitate renewal of the Church if they are advised and assisted by competent experts rather than by untrained but charismatic visionaries.

Let me remark further that in my remarks in this paper, I intend to do the best I can to forget that I am a priest, or even a Catholic, and to take a hard and critical look at the current organization of the Catholic Church as, let us say, an agnostic student of complex organizations might view the Church. This will enable me to speak with a frankness that might not otherwise be possible if I were afraid of treading on ecclesiastical toes.

1. *The Catholic Church in the world and in the United States has virtually no institution dedicated to research and planning.* There is probably no other large organization in the modern world that has less idea of what it is doing, how much it is accomplishing, or where it is going, than does the Catholic Church. Social research is, by and large, considered to be limited to the gathering of statistics, and terribly poor statistics, at that, are providing *ad hoc* answers to specific questions, usually as cheaply as possible. Scholars—social, historical, and theological—who could provide the raw material for research and policy-planning are frequently, indeed generally, viewed not with the respect and enthusiasm most large organizations have for their idea men, but with skepticism and suspicion. Information-gathering, which presumably is the absolute requisite for enlightened and intelligent decision-making, proceeds according to the most primitive and unreliable methods, and the policy-planning function which most complex modern organizations view as absolutely essential, hardly exists in the Catholic Church. Of course, if one contends that the Church need not adjust as the world around it changes, and that the work of the Church remains basically simple even though society grows

ever more complex, there is precious little need for research or policy-planning and the establishment of whatever long-range goals might be necessary can be effectively carried on by Ecumenical Councils. However, in the wake of the Vatican Council such an approach to research and planning within the Catholic Church simply does not appear to be tenable.

2. *It is not clear that the current methods of selecting leadership elites within the Church have produced the most competent or able administrators.* Unquestionably some ecclesiastical leaders are very able and equally unquestionably, some are incompetent. But any casual reader of, let us say, the history of the American Church, or even the daily press, cannot escape the conclusion that leaders who lack striking ability in the Church considerably out-number the less able leaders found in most other modern organizations. It also would seem that a considerable amount of administrative talent as well as policy-planning ability is over-looked in the Church because the people possessing this ability are not considered conservative enough to be "safe." But most research on social organization suggests that at least in the modern world, conservative leadership and safe leadership are not the same thing, and that in the long run the goals of an organization are best served by leadership that, while exercising proper precautions, is enlightened enough and progressive enough to create a sense of dynamic movement within its organization. The lack of a system of merit promotion within the Church, as well as the absence of a rigorous search for progressive and dynamic leadership must be listed as major organizational weaknesses of contemporary Catholicism.

3. An astute observer of contemporary society has made the following comment:

> The Dignity of the human person requires the right to act freely and responsibly. For this reason in social relations, man should exercise his rights, fulfill his obligations and in countless forms of collaboration with others act chiefly on his own responsibility and initiative. This is to be done in such a way that each one acts on his own decision of set purpose and from a consciousness of his obligation without being moved by force of pressure brought to bear on him externally.
>
> Where any human society is established on relations of force it must be regarded as inhuman inasmuch as the

personality of its members is repressed or restricted, when in fact they should be provided with appropriate incentive and means for developing and perfecting themselves.

John XXIII, *Pacem in Terris*, Article 34.

It's worth noting that the author of this statement is not a specialist in social organization. Nor is he a dreamy social radical. Rather, the principle of *professionalism* in the above paragraph was enunciated by John XXIII in his Encyclical letter *Pacem in Terris. The dispassionate student of contemporary Catholicism, however, is forced to note that there is not nearly enough professional initiative and responsibility within the Catholic Church.* The feudal relationships, for example, between pastor and curate, or between the religious superior and subjects, far from maximizing initiative and responsibility, seem rather to minimize it. In addition to violating what John XXIII would consider a basic human right, this absence of freedom of initiative and responsibility severely inhibits the efficiency of the Catholic Church. For only when men are free to exercise their initiative and to act on their own responsibility do they become capable of making the most intensive and constructive contributions to work in organizations to which they belong. The feudal relationships that continue between superior and subject (and even the words are unfortunate) within the Church are, one might almost say, worse than immoral. They are wasteful. One is further tempted to say that in the complexity of modern society only an organization which is preserved from complete disaster by the Holy Spirit could survive such unconscionable waste.

4. *Whatever theoretical advances that may have been made recently in our understanding of the nature of the Church as a collegial organization, it is difficult to observe very much of this collegiality operating in practice.* From a social organizational point of view, collegiality is necessary, not so much on moral grounds, but on sheer pragmatic grounds of efficiency. In an organization composed of educated, competent, and dedicated professionals, modern organizational theory holds that the collegial form of governance is easily the most effective. The collegial leader is occupied not so much with providing answers, but rather with asking the right questions of the right people; and he does not feel that his authority is weakened in the slightest because decisions are made after consultation and consensus rather than before. Thus, for example, John Kennedy did not lose any of his power or effectiveness as a leader because his decision and response to the Cuban missile crisis was the result of a collegial rather

than a unilateral decision. Neither, interestingly enough, was the power of the council of ministers of the Soviet Union at all weakened by the fact that their response to Kennedy's response was also, it would seem, collegial. For important matters in modern society, collegial decision-making is no longer optional, yet it would seem that in the face of this almost overwhelming fact, substantial portions of the leadership element within the Catholic Church are not persuaded that collegiality does not threaten their authority. From the viewpoint of social theory, it seems safe to say, the Catholic Church will not even begin to *be* in the modern world until it becomes far more collegial in its day-to-day operations. Unilateral paternalism may be an efficient way to run a Teutonic tribe, or perhaps even a naval ship in combat (though even this is not clear), but it is certainly not efficient for a complex modern organization.

5. *The Catholic Church not only does not have institutions for internal criticism, but, by and large, does not seem to encourage the existence of such institutions,* even though more recently and independently the press in the United States has begun to play a critical role, albeit without any special invitation. Almost any efficient modern corporation has at least one, and usually several, organs of criticism, either internally financed and staffed or provided by some outside organization. The role of such institutions is to be constantly supervising and questioning the techniques and methodology of the organization and the profession of management consultant has become a complex and elaborate one with many varieties of specialization within it. The modern organization argues that only when it is constantly being criticized and evaluated in an objective and impartial fashion can it be sure that its responses to the challenges of the world outside are all that they might be. As Kenneth Keniston has recently noted, democratic societies cannot be confident of survival unless the universities within these societies are free to play to the fullest the university role of social critic. The Catholic universities both in this country and the world have not been, generally speaking, encouraged to be critical, and institutions set up deliberately to carry on evaluation assignments simply do not exist. The dispassionate outside observer would almost be forced to conclude that the Catholic Church does not feel that it needs internal criticism because it does not feel that it is capable of making any serious organizational mistakes.

6. *Unlike the very considerable number of international organizations both public and private that have emerged in the last quarter of a century, the Catholic Church does not, save in a token fashion, recruit*

its administrative personnel internationally. One need not intend any criticism at all to the Italian people, the Italian clergy, or the Italian hierarchy, to say that it is dysfunctional for morale, and for the effective operation of the Catholic Church that the overwhelming professional international leadership seems to be Italian. An organization which has international problems must recognize that the canons of efficiency, if not equity, demand that its personnel also be international. Such internationalization of personnel in the past, of course, was impossible for reasons of transportation and communication, but surely in an age of transoceanic-telephonic communication and supersonic jet transports, such argumentation is no longer valid. Even though one hears frequently of the proposed reform in internationalization of the Roman curia, it must be noted that such internationalization seems not to be proceeding at the most rapid pace.

7. *Any effective and efficient modern organization realizes that it must provide responsibility for its personnel at as early an age as possible, and also have at least some relatively youthful personnel at the very highest level of leadership.* It goes without saying, of course, that even if the pastorate in its present canonical form were to be continued, the thirty-year wait for such a position of responsibility which most American priests, at least, must face, is fantastically inefficient. Furthermore, the dispassionate student of social organization must say that the Catholic Church fails to promote its most promising people to top level positions of responsibility at an early enough age. The problems in the environment which the Church faces, indeed which any modern organization faces, change so rapidly that the flexibility necessary to respond demands at least some youthful leadership. Thus the Nineteenth Century policy of men in their early thirties becoming bishops (Gibbons, Ireland, Keane, and Spalding, for example, were all bishops in their middle thirties), and archbishops in their early forties seemed to be a much more efficient way of assuring dynamic leadership than the present policy. It is interesting to note that, with one exception, none of the members of the 1960 Kennedy cabinet were old enough to be major leaders in the American Catholic Church or, indeed, to have top-level positions in the Roman curia. One surely does not intend to negate the wisdom of age and experience when one observes that the complete absence of youthful personnel at the top leadership level is an extraordinarily inefficient mode of operation. Similarly, one has to observe that the absence of any truly effective retirement policy would be incredible in any other complex organization. Only an organization protected by the Holy Spirit could survive leadership that is physically antiquated.

8. *Even though the documents of the Vatican Council placed emphasis on the needs of consultation and communication between the leadership elements and the rank and file, there is little evidence that organs to facilitate such communication have come into existence.* One has the impression that the general feeling is that such communication and consultation is useful and good, but can be approached at a somewhat leisurely pace. However, other modern organizations (including, one might note, military establishments of the various great powers) are convinced that consultation and communication are not optional but absolutely imperative and expend considerable time and resources in assuring themselves that their channels of communication are as functional as possible. The principle of the human-relations approach to management that holds "Everyone should be seriously consulted about the making of that decision whose cooperation is essential to the implementation of the decision" is not, it ought to be noted, intended as an ethical principle but as a pragmatic norm for effective behavior.

9. *The financial officers of banks who deal intensively with dioceses and religious communities usually have a vast repertoire of stories (most of them funny and many of them tragic) about the financial naiveté and incompetency of some religious leaders.* Unquestionably, many leaders are extraordinarily skillful in matters of finance, but recent public revelations also demonstrate that a fair number are naive and even incompetent. *The major problem is that no one can say for sure how much incompetency and how much competency there is, in the absence of a careful and standardized routine of fiscal supervision.* The financial procedures and policies of the Catholic Church are complete mysteries to everyone outside and to most of those inside. Indeed, many observers have come to suspect that they are mysteries even to most of those who presumably exercise financial control. A system of accounting and accountability not only to prevent disasters of the sort that recently reached the public press, but also to provide the immense savings that standardized financial practices make possible, is absolutely imperative in the Catholic Church. It is also extremely unlikely that such a system of accountability can be devised that could not be, in some fashion or other, public accountability.

10. Studies of the efficient operation of bureaucratic structures strongly suggest that in the absence of personal security, most professional staff members cannot operate efficiently, and furthermore, that those who must deal at least intermittently with professional bureaucracies cannot do so effectively unless there is some means by which they may appeal in

the arbitrary decisions that might be imposed upon them. *Thus, both the welfare of the professional and religious functionaries, as well as the rank and file members of the Church and (from the social organizational viewpoint, more importantly), the efficient operation of the organization demand that there be effective protection of the right of appeal*—a protection which generally would include the right of cross-examination, advice by counsel, security from anonymous denunciations, and publication of decisions and the reasons on which the decisions are based. It would be an exaggeration to say that there is no right of appeal in the Catholic Church, but the impression that a dispassionate outside observer would have is that few, if any, of the professional personnel in the Church believe that they will receive fair treatment from such appellate processes. Once again we must insist that emphases here are placed on the necessity of the right of appeal not so much on ethical grounds as on the purely pragmatic grounds of an efficient operation of a large organization in the complexities of contemporary life.

11. *Finally, the outside observer would lament the lack of sophisticated and competent public relations institutions within the Church.* He would think that such inefficiency was particularly dysfunctional at a time when the Church, without any effort of its own, seems to be obtaining huge amounts of publicity. Such publicity could quite readily enhance greatly the image of the Church in the mind of the non-Catholic public, but frequently, because of the inept public relations procedures, it harms rather than enhances the public image of the Church. An organization protected by the Holy Spirit can perhaps escape disaster, at least ultimate disaster, if it cares little or nothing about what others think of it, but one doubts very much if the Holy Spirit does any more than tolerate public relations ineptitude.

For purposes of emphasis, this paper has insisted on the social organizational weaknesses of the Catholic Church—the policies and practices that inhibit its efficient and effective functioning in the modern world. One does not, of course, argue that there is malice or bad will behind the policies and practices under discussion. Nor does one intend to deny that in almost every area we have mentioned action has already been taken and progress is being made. Nonetheless, it seems to me that our friend, the dispassionate outside observer, would simply not be able to understand why the action has been so hesitant and the progress has been so slow.

Personal and Organizational Effectiveness in the Roman Catholic Church

Donald P. Warwick

The task of this paper is to examine the implications of socio-psychological theory and research for improvements in the overall effectiveness of the Roman Catholic Church. In the subsequent discussion I would like to distinguish between two aspects of effectiveness: (1) organizational effectiveness, a term used by sociologists in describing the extent to which a group is achieving its collective goals; and (2) personal effectiveness, or the degree to which individual members of the Church are able to work toward their mission in the Church with the maximum possible freedom and dignity. The central issue to be considered here concerns the ways in which the Church as a large scale organization might both promote and draw benefits from the personal effectiveness of its members.

To begin, let us take up the question of organizational effectiveness. Despite the obvious importance of the subject, it is difficult to locate any material outlining the goals actually pursued by the Church in its day-to-day work. If a sample of theologians were asked about the

Mr. Donald Warwick received his doctorate in Social Psychology from the University of Michigan in 1963. He is presently a lecturer in Social Relations and Director of the Comparative International Program in the Department of Social Relations, Harvard University. Mr. Warwick was co-author of SHIFT WORK: THE SOCIAL, PSYCHOLOGICAL, AND PHYSICAL EFFECTS.

ultimate purpose of the Church, many would probably respond that it is the salvation of mankind through the teachings of Christ. For the social scientist an answer at this level of generality would not be terribly helpful because it is too far removed from the formal structure of the Church and the program which the institution supports. What is needed for the present type of analysis is a statement of the *penultimate* or *operational* goals of the Church, i.e., the broad classes of means chosen to reach the ultimate objective. Such a statement could also be translated into a set of criteria which could be used by the Church in appraising its current effectiveness.[1]

Since professional theologians and others more competent than I have failed to provide us with a workable framework of goals, it is necessary to do some improvisation. The list which follows is based upon general theories of organizational effectiveness, the objectives implied or stated in the recent Vatican Council, and various other writings on the role of the Church in the modern world. It should be noted that these are conceived as *ideal* objectives, and not necessarily those actually pursued by the leaders of the Church.

1. *Recruitment and retention of members who freely accept the Christian faith.* From an organizational viewpoint I would have to raise serious questions about the continuation of infant baptism as the principal *de facto* means of recruitment. Apart from any theological difficulties, this practice seems to have led to a false sense of accomplishment in the Church, as has the technique of mass conversions.

2. *Understanding and internalization of the values, beliefs, and moral standards of the faith.* The documents of Vatican II shattered forever the idealized image of the blind believer who accepts his faith much as he accepts his culture, unknowingly and unquestioningly. The newer emphasis is much more upon internal acceptance and conviction than upon external compliance.

3. *The formation of meaningful communities of believers.* The concept of community which seems to be developing in the modern Church is not a specific group of persons, but rather a quality of sharing and participation among individuals with common concerns. The Church, therefore, is not the same as community, but is rather a means of promoting a *koinonia* which may involve other groups as well.

---

1. Cf. Daniel Katz and Robert Kahn, *The Social Psychology of Organizations,* New York: John Wiley and Sons, 1966, Ch. 12.

4. *Individual action in the temporal order.* The Council documents dealing with the laity point out that it is the responsibility of members in the secular order to carry out their work in the light of a Christian conscience. While there seems to be an unresolved dualism between the sacred and secular realms in the Council statements, the implication is clear that the mission of the Church includes renewal of the temporal order through individual action.

5. *Effective internal administration.* The Church seems to be increasingly committed to modernization of its own administrative procedures and structures, including the Curia, Canon Law, and the extension of decision-making to the Synod of Bishops. Perhaps the most fundamental question to be considered in this paper concerns the ways in which internal administration can be used to advance the other goals noted here. It might be stated at the outset that the Church could well become more *efficient* in its managerial operations (a la General Motors) without becoming more *effective* in reaching its essential goals. In fact, it could be argued that increased efficiency may be harmful by prolonging the life of a moribund institutional structure.

6. *Adaptation to changing environmental conditions.* In the past the Church has shown a remarkable capacity to adapt itself to the requirements of certain ages. The present difficulty, however, is that the Church has so thoroughly wedded itself to the metaphysics, bureaucratic structures, and political style of medieval monarchies that change is a painfully slow process. The experience of other organizations suggests that successful adaptation requires constant planning for change, and that effective planning requires personnel specialized in this function. One starting point in the Church's planning might be an honest and realistic analysis of the extent of historical conditioning in its present organizational structures.

This review of goals underscores one point on which the Church differs drastically from the majority of organizations: the intimate and reciprocal relationship between personal and organizational effectiveness. Unlike the typical corporate bureaucracy, the Church cannot claim success if it records an annual profit on its investments, gains a larger share of the available "market," and functions with a smoothly operating administrative apparatus. Not many years ago some Churchmen took considerable pride in the fact that the international operations of Catholicism were given an efficiency rating about on a par with Standard Oil. While no one can deny that the Vatican could learn a great deal from Standard Oil, in many respects this rating should have been a cause for concern rather than joy. In fact, the lesson of history seems to be that the Church reached the pinnacle of personal and organizational effectiveness in the first days of its existence, precisely at a time when it had none of the trappings of formal bureaucracy. In the succeeding centuries the priorities of the gospel have been inverted to the point that countless Christians, be they priests, religious, or laymen, must daily sacrifice their own dignity, freedom, and sometimes integrity in the service of an authoritarian administrative system. Such conditions cannot continue, and call for a thoroughgoing reform in the very conception of the Church and its institutional expression.

As one step toward such a reform, we might ask how the Roman Catholic Church can modify its organizational structures and procedures to advance both personal and organizational effectiveness. The remainder of this paper will be devoted to five interrelated aspects of this question: (1) the uses and limitations of formal organization; (2) the structure of authority, leadership, and law; (3) the central administration of the Church; (4) the role of the clergy; and (5) the Church and the layman. To meet the purposes of the present Symposium the emphasis will be upon short and medium-range changes, rather than upon some ultimate ideal definition of the Church.

Uses and Limits of Formal Organization

Probably the most basic *sociological* problem facing the Church is that of reconciling the incompatibilities of community and formal organization. It is apparent that the Church today is extremely fragile on the dimensions of community and meaning, and that these qualities will have to be actively promoted if it is to be more than a ritualistically oriented membership group. It is equally apparent, however, that some type of formal organization or bureaucracy (in its technical sense) will be needed to allow the Church to function in the modern world. The root question therefore, is *how much* organization and *what types* can be used not only to improve the administrative machinery of the Church, but also to promote community and spontaneity.

Theories of large-scale organizations suggest that the characteristics required in an efficient bureaucracy are largely incompatible with those of a Christian community. From the time of Max Weber formal organizations have been seen as a rational ordering of *functions* to serve certain foreordained ends. Most of the literature presently available deals with the organization of functions for economic productivity, military efficiency, or governmental administration. Persons fit into the organization only insofar as they fulfill the necessary functions, and in carrying out their duties they are expected to adhere to established rules, be emotionally neutral to clients, and in other ways to limit their individual propensities. More recent theories have emphasized the importance of meaningful personal relationships on the job and especially in work groups, but even these are viewed as means-to-ends. Also, recent research suggests that warm and cohesive group relationships in the factory or office do not necessarily lead to greater productivity, and may sometimes work against this end. Thus the current approach is to foster cohesive groups whose norms are compatible with those of the administration.

The goals of the Church, on the other hand, necessitate communities in which members are regarded as persons rather than employees, where great value is placed upon the unique qualities of the individual and the meaning of the faith to him, and where there are deep bonds of emotional solidarity.[2] I would submit that these types of relationships are largely antithetical to the norms of the large bureaucracy.

Here then, we see the sociological dilemma in the contemporary Roman Catholic Church. Given its highly centralized structure, the demands for new services arising from the Second Vatican Council, and pressures from all sides for the modernization of its operations, the Vatican will in all likelihood retain most of the elements of formal organization which it now possesses, and add others. This palatine modernization process will be justified on the grounds that it will enable the Church to "do more," and do it better. However, a latent effect of increased centralization (and ironically, perhaps, of better services from the Vatican) will be a continued and geometrically progressive decay of the sense of community in the Church, reflected in widespread defections of clergy, religious, and laity. To forestall this development, it is not necessary for the Church to sell the Vatican State and close its administrative operations completely. What is needed, however, is a drastic reduction in the scale of these operations, and the creative use of human organization to promote rather than restrict creativity, spontaneity, and community among Christians. The Pope and the

---

2. The literature of Sociology is replete with discussions of the qualities of relationships in differing types of groups. The writings of Talcott Parsons in this area, especially on the subject of pattern variables, are especially valuable, although too detailed for present purposes.

Bishops of the world must come to see that the present organizational deficiencies of the Church will not be solved by new congregations and added bureaucratic layers.

One immediate recommendation is that the Church should undertake an intensive and unbiased study of the appropriateness of its present structure for its overall goals. It is quite likely that such a study would lead to the conclusion that various offices in Rome could be abolished, and that the number of layers or "clearance-points" in the system could be lessened. Interestingly enough, the experience of the Administrative Area of the U.S. Department of State shows that it is possible to reduce the scale of bureaucracy by as many as 6-8 levels of supervision without seriously impairing the efficiency of the system. An evaluation of these changes in which I participated showed that in many cases the reorganized units were carrying out more work *per man* after the reorganization than before. This experiment points up several leads for the Church as well.

Structure of Authority, Leadership and Law

Modern organizational research suggests that if the Church is to be effective in reaching its major goals, the exercise of authority will have to be *de-papalized* and *de-clericalized*.

It would not be difficult to conclude from the teachings of the not-too-distant past that the Church *is* the Pope and the clergy, and that laymen serve as a kind of necessary Third Order. While the theology of the Church is now explicit in its attribution of integral roles to all members, the structures of authority, leadership, and law convey a somewhat different picture. Let me comment briefly on each of these three topics.

AUTHORITY

Various studies indicate that authority relationships and control processes in an organization have a strong bearing upon its overall effectiveness.[3] A fairly general finding in Western organizations is that productivity and member identification tend to be *lowest* when authority is heavily concentrated at the top of the organization, and when the techniques of control are mainly coercive or semi-coercive (physical danger,

---

3. See, for example, Rensis Likert, *New Patterns of Management*, New York: McGraw-Hill, 1961.

threats of dismissal, etc.). This general trend seems to be especially true in the case of voluntary organizations and other groups which are more "member-oriented" than "production-oriented."

It is evident that the contemporary Church, even with the Council reforms, meets the requirements for limited effectiveness. The doctrines of the Church make it exceedingly clear that the fullness of its authority is vested in the Pope, and recent Pontiffs have reiterated their belief in the supreme powers of this office. Moreover, the central administration of the Church has traditionally found itself quite comfortable with means of control that are at least semi-coercive, including suppression of writings, removal from office, and threats of excommunication.

To correct this situation there must first be a *radical de-emphasis on the role of the Pope, both in theory and in practice, and a large-scale decentralization of authority.* It is difficult to see how this change can be made in the present Church, since all of the decision-making procedures are ultimately subject to papal approval or veto. But, whatever the means, it seems absolutely vital to reduce the distance between the top and the bottom of the Church as an organization. Such a step would serve not only to foster a greater sense of community in the Church, but also to increase the efficiency of its administrative apparatus. The role of Pope as presently defined seems to be much more a vestige of the Church's days as a medieval monarchy than a product of the teachings of the Gospel.

Some of the specific actions that might be adopted to reduce the prominence of the Papacy in the Church would include the following:

1. *Adoption of a limited term of office for the Pope.* From an organizational viewpoint it is unwise to entrust the leadership of the Church to one man for an indefinite period, especially when his term of office may span two or three decades. The Pope himself recently set a limit of five years on appointments to the Curia: is there any reason why the same policy should not be applied to his own office? While this proposal has obvious drawbacks (e.g., the presence of several retired successors of Peter), it might have the advantage of providing for younger and more dynamic leadership in the Church. In human terms the College of Cardinals might occasionally vote for a man of 40 if they knew that they could vote him out in 5 or even 10 years. Perhaps a term of 10 years, renewable at the discretion of the electoral body would be a reasonable interim measure.

2. *Re-casting the role of the Pope in Catholic theology.*

While it will undoubtedly be necessary to retain some form of ultimate legitimate authority in the Church, it would be advisable to reconsider the scope of this authority and the theological terms in which it is expressed. Given the value patterns of modern man, the Pope might be more effective as a spiritual leader if he were gradually to become the Invisible Head of the Church. More specifically, Catholic theology should simply mention the role of the Pope less frequently, and change the terms in which it is expressed. I suspect that most men of today cringe at the use of phrases such as "Supreme Pontiff," and do not wish to be constantly reminded of his absolute authority in the Church. Would it not be more in keeping with the spirit of the Gospels if the Popes were to adopt a more humble posture and abrogate the vocabulary and manners of the medieval monarchy? Would anything of real significance be lost if the encyclicals were stripped of their formalism and expressed in the simple direct style that characterizes contemporary society? Given the encrusted traditions of the Papacy, such changes would be difficult to make, but they would also contribute greatly to the promotion of a sense of community among the members of the Church. At the very least they would remove a major irritant to all Christians.

3. *Broadening the base of authority in decision-making.* At the present time the Pope has no obligation to consult anyone before making a major decision affecting the Church. One of the major reforms needed if the Church is to improve its effectiveness is an extension of this decision-making power to a broader group, such as the Synod of Bishops. The emphasis upon the absolute character of the Pope's authority is, after all, of relatively recent origins, and seems to be at variance with the more democratic traditions of the early Church. While a long-range goal might be a system in which decision-making is spread widely throughout the Church,[4] for the immediate future it would be helpful to aim for an extension of *real* authority to the Synod of Bishops. As presently constituted this body has no authority, and can be convened only at the request of the Pope. The Church, which in this case means the Pope, would be well-advised to endow the Synod with power, and to make it a permanent part of its decision-making procedures.

A second broad recommendation is that *the Church reduce the scope of control over its members, and rely mainly on persuasive rather than semi-coercive means of control.* In concrete terms, the Church should

---

4. For a possible model of this system cf. Rensis Likert, *Human Organization,* New York: McGraw-Hill, 1957.

attempt to regulate a smaller portion of the lives of Catholics, especially the clergy and religious, and when regulation is necessary use means aimed as convincing rather than forcing compliance. The day should quickly pass when priests or religious are threatened with removal from office or similar censures for expressing their honest views on matters related to the faith.

LEADERSHIP

Closely bound up with the question of authority is that of leadership. For purposes of this paper we may say that authority deals with the broad powers required to accomplish the work of an organization, while leadership refers to the influence of individuals on organization goals. Leadership usually depends upon some type of formal authority, but also draws upon other resources such as personal attractiveness.

Katz and Kahn, in *The Social Psychology of Organizations,* refer to three major types of leadership: (1) *origination,* or changing, creating, and eliminating organizational structures; (2) *interpolation,* or filling out incomplete structures; and (3) *administration,* i.e., the application of prescribed policies to predictable problems. It would seem that the Roman Catholic Church, like many traditional bureaucracies, has devoted too few of its energies to the first and too many to the last. The implications are serious, for, as Katz and Kahn observe: "The inability to alter and originate structures is perhaps an inconspicuous disease of leadership. . . . Nevertheless, in the long run the disease is absolutely fatal to organizations."[5]

Considering the fundamental importance of origination, we might ask how this type of leadership can be encouraged in the Church. The first requirement is the recruitment of leaders who are themselves relatively "open" in their personalities rather than individuals who derive neurotic satisfaction from the apparent immutability of ecclesiastical structures. Then a type of training should be given which provides potential leaders with a broad perspective on the relationship between the Church and its environment. Such training preferably offered in natural settings, rather than in monastic isolation should engender a dynamic sense of the constant interchange between the Church and the surrounding society, and a deep sensitivity to the movements of history and culture. Finally, the effective Church leader must be given ample latitude for experimentation with struc-

---

5. Katz and Kahn, *op. cit.,* p. 318.

tures, and should not be condemned to ignominy if some of his experiments fail.

LAW

An immediate task facing the Church administrators is the revision of the Code of Canon Law. In the light of statements made earlier about increasing the sense of community and spontaneity in the Church, I would offer the following as points for consideration in this effort. First, is it necessary for the Church to formulate its own body of *laws* rather than a set of modifiable administrative procedures? One clear drawback in a Code of Canon Law is that it immediately requires a corps of canon lawyers for its interpretation and enforcement. This requirement not only adds another cluster of bureaucratic positions to the organization of the Church, but also surrounds its administrative procedures with an aura of secrecy and exclusion. The aim of the Church at this juncture in history should be to make its operation as intelligible as possible to all members, and a separate set of laws would seem to work against this end.

Secondly, if the Code of Canon Law is retained, it would be very wise to reduce its scope, especially on matters related to clergy and religious. The ideal of this type of law should be to set down a minimum of basic working principles which restrict individuals as little as possible, and promote their rights as members of the organization.

Central Administration of the Church

It is paradoxical that the encyclicals of the Church have strongly endorsed the principle of subsidiarity in economic and political life, while its own administration has moved in the opposite direction. Given its overall goals, the Church today remains over-centralized, and should grant much more authority and autonomy to its national or at least regional divisions.

There are at least two ways in which such a shift would contribute to the effectiveness of the Church. First, at the psychological level this change would reduce the feeling on the part of members, both clerical and lay, that the *real* Church is "over there" and controlled by "foreigners." As I indicated earlier, various studies suggest that the greater the perceived distance, both spatial and psychological, between members and elites, the less the feeling of identification on the part of members. The internationalization of the Curia might help to reduce some of the feelings of distance, but it is a far less potent change than outright decentralization. A second advantage of decentralized control is greater flexibility in adapting the structure, teachings, and worship of the Church to widely varying cultural situaations. It would be apparent to almost any cultural anthropologist that the policies set in Rome for the Universal Church have been guided by a deep and pervasive ethnocentrism. On a whole array of questions, especially in the field of liturgy and missionary methods, the Church in Rome would do well to initiate a decade of experimentation in which basic decisions were left to national or regional episcopal conferences. Some steps in this direction have already been made, and more should be encouraged.

The Role of the Clergy

In addition to a de-emphasis upon the status of the Papacy and a major decentralization of administrative functions, two of the most needed changes in the Church today are the eradication of clericalism, and the simultaneous development of a more flexible clergy. Both of these steps, I feel, would greatly advance the formation of a unified and meaningful Christian community, and remove certain obstacles to personal effectiveness among clergy and laity alike, Since they might seem to be rather inconsistent recommendations, let me comment briefly on each.

CLERICALISM[6]

The history of the clergy in the Roman Catholic Church might be summarized as a period of relatively low differientiation of priests and laymen, followed by the establishment of a priestly caste in the postconstantinian era, and then the recent halting steps toward declericalization. However, despite the desire of many individual clerics to lessen their separation from the rest of the Christian people, there are still many signs of doctrines and policies which reinforce the caste mentality. Perhaps the most important at the theological level is the concept of an "indelible mark" on the soul of the priest. Such a permanent form of identification is standard in all caste systems, and serves to indicate the intrinsic separation of one group from the rest. And, like many ancient societies, the Church also relies upon distinctive dress, titles, manners, language (Latin), the monopoli-

6. An excellent treatment of this topic is found in J. Blenkinsopp, "On Clericalism," *Cross Currents,* 17, 1, 1967, pp. 15-23.

zation of worship and moral teaching, and even celibacy as further means of differentiating the priest from the ordinary believer. In short, considering the history of the Church and other traditional societies, it would be fair to conclude that the role of the priest as presently defined is largely a vestige of medieval clericalism, and ill-adapted to the needs of the modern Church.

As Blenkinsopp[7] points out in his discussion of clericalism, the irony of this development is that it is so completely at variance with the figure of Christ and with the experience of the early Church. Christ Himself was a layman in the religion of his birth, and an ardent opponent of the priestly class and the type of religion which they dispensed. Similarly, in the New Testament there is no evidence of the elevation of the clergy which reached full bloom in the Middle Ages, and which persists in many ways today. Blenkinsopp observes that

"... Nowhere in the New Testament is any individual Christian ever referred to as priest. The usual explanation—that the use of the word would have created confusion with the priesthood of the old order—is only half of the truth. Much more important is the insistence that no new caste arise in the community to take the place of the old." (p. 17)

It would be a mistake to attribute all of the ills of the Church to clericalism, but it is also difficult to escape the conclusion that the growth of a priestly class has been a serious obstacle to mature spirituality. One of the natural by-products of the monopolization of worship is the tendency to place greater value on form than on intention in the liturgy, and to encourage dependency and passivity on the part of the faithful. These trends have been amply documented in the Roman Catholic Church, and have contributed to the loss of almost all spontaneity in the Catholic worship.

Whether or not one agrees with this brief historical analysis, the point to be made here is that the Church of today requires a group of priests who are much closer to their fellow Christians, and who are not set apart by accidentals such as titles and dress. If there is to be a growth of meaningful community in the Church,

"The priest will have to be seen as a person chosen to carry out a function within, not above or apart from the community, and a function, moreover, which is nothing but a specialization

---

7. *loc. cit.*

of that community as a whole. He is one of the people, a lay-man to whom a special job has been entrusted."[8]

The specific changes I would recommend as immediate steps are in large part those which are being carried out unofficially by younger priests in the United States and parts of Europe. These include the abandon-ment of a distinctive clerical garb, foresaking the title of "Father" or its equivalent, and a general willingness to participate as an equal in the in-formal events of the Christian community and the "secular city." In addi-tion, a radical change is needed in the theology of the priesthood, especially on the issues of the "indelible mark." Such a concept is both a metaphysi-cal absurdity (even St. Thomas held that the substantial form of man is ink-resistant) and a psychological barrier to the fulfillment of the goal of community.

TOWARD A MORE FLEXIBLE CLERGY

To increase its effectiveness in modern society the Church must adopt a conception of the priesthood that is much more free and flex-ible than the present model, and much less socially elevated. Perhaps, as Ivan Illich has suggested in his stimulating discussion of "The Vanishing Clergyman,"[9] the prototypical priest of the future will fulfill his ministry on a part-time basis, and will be like a layman in most other respects. These proposals have much to commend them, and should be seriously considered in any long-range planning efforts. But for the immediate future we must also ask how the Church can improve the policies governing its full-time professional clergy, both to provide better service to the larger Christian community, and to eliminate the many injustices and indignities suffered by priests throughout the world. I cannot agree with Illich that the optimal solution is to let the present abuses continue, and thereby encourage a mass exodus of clergymen which will, in turn, stimulate a more profound re-appraisal of the priesthood than is presently possible. With the current rate of defections among the clergy and the decline in vocations throughout the world, the Church *will* initiate changes within the next decade, and it is important that these changes be for the good of all concerned.

What, then, are some of the specific reforms that might be undertaken to develop a more flexible and effective clergy? Research on

8. Blenkinsopp, *op. cit.*, p. 16.
9. CIF Reports, Cuernavaca, Mexico, 1967.

the sociology of occupations points up possibilities, and I would suggest a few others that might be considered on an experimental basis.

1. *Focusing of recruitment efforts on mature individuals with experience in the secular society.* By almost any standard the policy of recruiting students of high-school age for training in minor seminaries has been a failure. The Church should follow the lead of almost all other organizations which seek candidates only from the adult population (18 or over), and expect some prior training in secular institutions. To be able to attract such persons in sufficient numbers the Church will have to effect drastic changes in the image of the priests and conditions of employment through steps such as those which follow.

2. *Adaption of training to occupational requirements.* The results of the Fichter Survey are relevant to this point:

> "The central finding here is that these respondents report inadequate career preparation for the very functions that absorb most of their time and energy. They are constantly dealing with people, serving them as other Christs, and yet they complain that they had practically no training in social relations."[10]

It might be added that the approved curricula in major seminaries accurately reflects the Church's emphasis on hierarchy, obedience, law, procedures, and conformity in dogma. If there is to be a greater movement toward the goal of meaningful community in the Church, and if more attention is to be paid to the pastoral rather than juridical role of the priest, profound reforms will be necessary in seminary education. There is good reason to suggest, in fact, that the long-range plans of the Church should call for exclusive reliance upon established educational institutions (preferably secular) for undergraduate education, and the transfer of theological training to a few high-quality seminaries covering much wider geographic areas than at present.

3. *Consideration of individual preferences and abilities in the assignment process.* To aid in the development of a high level of motivation among the clergy, Bishops should solicit the assignment preferences of each priest, and be guided by these statements in decisions on placement.

---

10. J. Fichter, "The Fichter Survey—implications and interpretations," *National Catholic Reporter,* August 2, 1967, p. 6.

A more radical proposal suggested by the experience of other organizations is a shifting of the "employment market" for priests from the diocesan to the provincial or even national level. Under this plan candidates for the priesthood would enter a major seminary with no formal commitment to a specific diocese. In the last year of their training they would establish contact with interested Bishops, and arrange conditions of employment that were mutually agreeable. Despite its practical difficulties, such a system would have many advantages from a social-psychological point of view. First, in view of the scarcity of candidates, Bishops would be forced to give explicit attention to needs and preferences of priests hired for their Diocese. Moreover, they would be less inclined to deal with them in an arbitrary and authoritarian manner, for the latter would always retain the option of moving to another Diocese. Second, the priest in this situation would have no guarantee of continued employment unless a kind of tenure system were arranged. I am quite aware of the problems entailed in this proposal, especially in view of present incardination and excardination requirements and the organization of the Church's administration on a diocesan basis. However, this proposal or at least some of its components should be given serious study before the employment policies of the Church are frozen in a revised Canon Law.

4. *Democratization of the relationships between senior and junior priests.* The development of a professionally-oriented priesthood would require basic changes in the authority relationships between senior and junior priests in the parish and elsewhere. The younger clergy should be given the same freedom and responsibility that is common to other professions and should be included as full participants in the process of decision-making. While there is little doubt that changes in this direction will be more the result of education than of Church edict, a few practical steps might be suggested: (1) greater reliance on "team" assignments in which no one is formally designated as pastor, and decision-making is carried out collectively; (2) specification of the professional rights of curates in future statements of Canon Law or its successor; and (3) re-definition of the role of pastor, both in theology and in law, to place greater emphasis upon the ideal of *primus inter pares.*

5. *Improved avenues of career mobility, especially through merit promotions.* To bring itself more into line with the larger society, the Church should adopt a personnel system in which there is less of a separation between pastors and curates, and in which promotion to the pas-

torate is based upon achievement rather than seniority. This proposal has already been well-elaborated in the writings of Fichter and Greeley.

The Church and the Layman

It would be rather easy to conclude this paper with a few sentences lending the weight of organizational research to the movement for lay participation. But such an ending would be fundamentally misleading, for it would implicitly endorse a view of the layman which is truncated and increasingly irrelevant, i.e., the image of the organizationally active Christian. What I would prefer to do is examine the role of the ordinary Catholic in the total context of the Church's mission, and ask what might be done to assist him in fulfilling this role.

The recent Vatican Council described the Church in the modern World as the Pilgrim People of God. The contemporary layman must indeed be a pilgrim, but one who carries on his journey largely in solitude rather than in the company of a clan of believers. At times he re-joins the band for sustenance and sharing, but he must soon depart. And as a pilgrim he is so absorbed in the search for meaning in his wanderings that he can spare little enthusiasum for the inner workings of a remote and immobile Institutional Church.

In other words, the emerging layman of today is much more concerned with the significance of faith for his existence than with participation in parish councils, school boards, and similar structures. He would undoubtedly admit to the value of such efforts, and might even assume office if asked to do so. Still, the main questions are those which center about the persistent problems of identity, belief, and Christian relevance in modern society. He would welcome help from the Church on these issues, not through dogmatic instruction in the tenets of the latest encyclical, but by providing "inputs" that are of use in evolving his own solutions. At the same time, he is increasingly aware of the fact that there are others outside the Church who share in his quest, and with whom he experiences genuine elements of community.

It is dangerous, therefore, to regard heightened internal participation and expression almost as ends in themselves, without relating them to the simultaneous need for extra-institutional secular involvement. Unfortunately the bulk or organizational research has focused on the utilitarian question of how to increase member identification with a particular

106

group. In the case of the Church we must also ask how heightened participation and identification affect Christian commitment in the diaspora.

INTERNAL PARTICIPATION

From a practical standpoint there is little doubt that the Roman Catholic Church must increase the degree of lay participation in decision-making if it is to survive. The Church has always had to adapt itself to the prevailing norms in the realms of authority and political structures, and these norms now include decided emphasis upon democratic procedures and two-way influence. To bring about changes in this direction it must simultaneously decrease the prominence and authority of the upper levels of the hierarchy and expand the influence of its lower levels.

I would suggest as a general guideline *that laymen (male and female) be included in all of the major spheres of decision-making in the Church, including the parish, the diocese, the national conference, the Vatican, and even future ecumenical councils.* Moreover, the range of issues in which they are involved should embrace the core areas of moral and doctrinal development as well as the more mundane tasks of finances and routine administration. Whatever the specific organizational mechanisms used, the ideal would not be that of a quota system specifying a fixed percentage of laymen regardless of their competence, but an effective means of soliciting informed opinion and qualified employees from all quarters of the Church.

At some future date the Church might even experiment with a truly democratic system in which all members have some part in the election of Bishops and the Pope himself. The movement toward popular election of Bishops would be no wild innovation, as it was a common practice in the first few centuries of the Church. In a similar vein, there is no intrinsic theological justification for the election of the Pope by the College of Cardinals.

Finally, the Church could benefit greatly from the establishment of open channels for the expression of public opinion within its entire membership. One means might be a small but permanent office of research in the Vatican and in each national conference. Through the use of scientific methods of sampling and other standard research procedures an office of this type could collect information which would lead to more rational decisions by the central authorities, and at the same time increase the feelings of membership participation in the Church.

SECULAR INVOLVEMENT

My main hesitation about suggesting means of increased lay participation is that they might be successful, and thereby make the Church a more comfortable and attractive haven in a bewildering world. The Church can no longer be a nurturant human Mother, for the paramount task facing her sons is finding the relevance of the Gospels in their secular existence. Moreover, educated Christians are rapidly discovering that the most imaginative and meaningful approaches to social change have emerged from secular thought, and that the Church's halting forays into the World are often a source of embarrassment. Even the more progressive social encyclicals of Leo, Pius XI, John and Paul often seem to represent a bland synthesis of the humanist principles of the previous decade, and in an effort to present "answers" sometimes foreclose discussion at the point where it should begin.

If our aim is to devise means through which the Church might assist the layman to seek self-expression in the temporal world, the first suggestion might well be to do nothing officially. The time has arrived when the Catholic Church must cease pretending that she has the solutions to the perplexing problems confronting modern man. A welcome development from the viewpoint of many laymen would be a moratorium on official pronouncements, including encyclicals and edicts from the various Curial Offices. The educated Christian has tired of warnings about the dangers of modernism and exhortations against dangerous innovations. What he would appreciate at this point is some assistance in discovering the meaning of the Gospel for this and future societies, including full freedom to form unstructured communities of believers and non-believers, and to introduce a greater spontaneity into the liturgy. The price of such freedom may be a period of ecclesiological confusion, but would this be worse than the sterile and hollow conformity which now prevails?

CONCLUSIONS

My aim in this paper has been to examine the possible ways in which the Roman Catholic Church might increase both its organizational effectiveness and the personal effectiveness of its members. I have tried to show that the very nature of the Church demands that organizational structures and procedures should not be self-serving and self-perpetuating, but should rather be used as an instrument of promoting individual initiative and a sense of community among Christians. To reach these ends there must be a shift to a system which places much less emphasis upon the papacy, hierarchical authority, clerical prerogatives and juridical procedures and which consciously aims at fostering creativity, spontaneity, and freedom in the application of the Gospels to modern life. Several concrete recommendations were offered regarding means of effecting these changes.

There are two points that I would like to stress in closing. First, the Roman Catholic Church must begin to take seriously its teaching that the work of Christ is accomplished largely through the activity of individual Christians in the temporal order. There is still a strong current of feeling among many churchmen supporting the notion that the effective Catholic is one who is visibly active in one or more of the organizational offshoots of the Institutional Church. Thus an inordinate amount of the material and human resources of the institution are devoted to the establishment and maintenance of "in-house" activities which are of little or no value to the Christian working mainly in a secular setting. Second, the Church must also realize that the scale and type of its activities at the institutional level can be a positive hindrance and an embarrassment to clergy and laymen working mainly with non-Catholics. Among the more glaring examples would be the mysterious investment policies of the Vatican, the establishment of concordats, and the use of diplomatic recognition for highly questionable purposes, especially in "Catholic" countries such as Spain and Peru. The Church will have to learn that its organizational face is even more visible and vulnerable in the puplic eye than the official image it attempts to create through encyclicals and works of charity. In true evangelical fashion, the present Church is judged by its fruits, and not only nor mainly by those placed on public exhibit.

Although it represents an extreme point of view, there is considerable wisdom in the following statement by Ceslaus Hoinacki and Ivan Illich:[11]

"Now the Church must withdraw from all such specific

---

11. Ceslaus Hoinacki and Ivan Illich, "Religious Orders and Crisis." Cuernavaca, Mexico, *The Center for Intercultural Documentation,* 1967, pp. 5-6.

social initiative and involvement. This may be painful and, to some, scandalous. Recently, the Church has made hesitant and halting attempts to use her moral prestige and political power for seemingly revolutionary social persuasion. If the Church were suddenly to withdraw her institutional force for motivating and directing social options, one can easily imagine the liberal's howl of pain and the conservative's hurrah of glee. But the issue must be faced: If the Church continues to use her power and prestige in the social arena, she perpetuates her inability to witness to that which is specific and unique in her mission today. The Church's task is to evangelize men, not to socialize them. Living in contemporary society, her mission is to help man discover the transcendent meaning of life in this society —the meaning of change for the Christian. . . ."

In sum, the time has now arrived when Organizational Christianity must decrease so that Individual Christianity may increase.

IV.

AN HISTORICAL PERSPECTIVE

Roots of

Western Constitutionalism

in the Church's Own Tradition

The Significance of the Council of Constance

Brian Tierney

The legislation of the Council of Constance represents the only attempt during the past thousand years to establish a "constitutional" or "representative" system of government for the Roman Catholic church.[1] The decree *Haec sancta* declared that a General Council representing the church militant was the highest organ of ecclesiastical government. The decree *Frequens* declared that General Councils were to meet at regular, specified intervals in the future to carry through a far-reaching reform of the church in head and members. In the past few years a vigorous discussion has grown up among historians and theologians about the validity and significance of

1. In preparing this paper I have drawn on several of my published writings dealing with aspects of medieval conciliarism, namely *Foundations of the Conciliar Theory* (Cambridge, 1955); "Ockham, the Conciliar Theory and the Canonists," *Journal of the History of Ideas*, 15 (1954), 40-70; "Pope and Council: Some New Decretist Texts," *Mediaeval Studies*, 19 (1957), 197-218; "Canon Law and Western Constitutionalism," *Catholic Historical Review*, 52 (1966), 1-17; "Hermeneutics and History: The Problem of *Haec Sancta*," *Essays in Honor of Bertie Wilkinson* (Toronto, 1967).

Mr. Brian Tierney is a professor of History at Cornell University. He is a leading scholar of the medieval period, and, in particular, of the canon law of the middle ages. Mr. Tierney taught for several years at Catholic University of America, and was president of the American Catholic Historical Association in 1965.

these decrees. The historians are interested in them most of all as documents of major importance in the evolution of western representative institutions while the theologians are asking whether they embody any permanent truths about the intrinsic nature of the Christian church.[2]

These discussions are, perhaps, of more than mere academic interest. In modern times the structure of ecclesiastical government in the Catholic church has become radically alien to the central tradition of Western constitutionalism that the church itself did so much to foster during the Middle Ages. To many Christians the situation seems scandalous. But attempts to change it are often resisted as attacks on a divinely ordained pattern of government that has characterized the church through all the ages. In these circumstances a reconsideration of the Council of Constance and its antecedents may provide a useful background for the discussion of our modern problems.

Antecedents

Fifty years ago it was generally assumed that the decrees of Constance made a sharp break with all preceding ecclesiastical tradition and that they could be understood only as a perverse, panic-stricken response to the crisis of the Great Schism. The English historian, Figgis, for instance, maintained that *Haec sancta* was "the most revolutionary official document in the history of the world." He thought that the Conciliarists invented a novel theory of church government by merely imitating the experiments with representative institutions that had already taken place in several secular states. The theoretical writings of the Conciliarists, Figgis conceded, were of the highest importance in the subsequent growth of Western constitutionalism but, so far as the Catholic church itself was concerned, they were merely a momentary aberration after "the divine authority of a thousand years."[3]

We now know that *Haec sancta* was anything but revolutionary. The remote origins of the conciliar theory are to be found in those scriptural and patristic texts which referred to Peter's primacy as a function exercised within a collegiate government of all the apostles, and to that government in turn as functioning within a community of the faithful who participated actively in ecclesiastical decisions. And a more immediate

---

2. A useful introduction to the modern literature is provided by A. Franzen, "The Council of Constance: Present State of the Problem," *Concilium*, 7 (1965), 29-68.
3. J. N. Figgis, *From Gerson to Grotius*, 2nd ed. (Cambridge 1916), 41-70.

starting-point for the medieval tradition of conciliar thought is provided by the vast compilation of canonical texts assembled in Gratian's Decretum, the foundation of the medieval science of canon law (c. 1140).

A major tension in canonical thought arose from the fact that Gratian, like other medieval authors, used the same term, *potestas clavium,* to designate both the supreme juridical authority inhering in the papacy and also the power to remit sins, to "bind and loose," that was diffused throughout the priesthood.[4] The Decretists resolved the tension by formulating a concept of the church essentially similar to the doctrine of collegiality recently defined at Vatican Council II. They maintained that Christ conferred authority on all the apostles but also designated Peter as their head by promising to him in the first place, *pro omnibus et prae omnibus,* the "power of the keys" that was later conferred on all. But the Decretists went further than Vatican II in emphasizing that the subject of the indefectibility, the unfailing faith, which Christ had promised to His Church, was not Peter alone, nor even the apostolic college alone, but rather the whole congregation of the faithful. Thus Huguccio wrote, "In the person of Peter the church was understood, in the faith of Peter the faith of the universal church." And, again, "Wherever there are good faithful people, there is the Roman church."[5]

The Decretists were not theologians, content to explicate and contemplate the mystery of the church's being. They were jurists whose task was to define a structure of constitutional law appropriate to the church's intrinsic nature. There is, after all, no detailed scheme of constitutional organization for the church set out in the pages of the New Testament. The Scriptures give us only the barest essentials. Every age has had to fill in the details by calling on its own understanding of how societies can best be organized. The most sophisticated juridical principles known to the 12th century Decretists were those of classical Roman law and so they used those principles to the full in shaping the constitutional law of the medieval church. But, in using them, they adapted them in radically new ways. For instance, the Decretists employed details of Roman law relating to the ancient Senate in defining the functions and privileges of the cardinalate, an institution without any real basis in Scripture. More importantly they applied doctrines of Roman law to the papal office itself. It is well known that the canonists developed a theory of juridical sovereignty out of the old doctrine of papal headship by applying to the pope

---

4. Compare, e.g., C.24 q.1 *dictum post* c.4 and Dist. 20 *dictum ante* c.1.
5. On these canonical doctrines see *Foundations*, 36-46.

maxims like *Princeps legibus solutus est* and *Quod principi placuit legis habet vigorem.* Equally important and less well known is the fact that they also sought to explicate the concept of collegiality in terms of Roman law—and that, in doing so, they developed constitutional ideas of the highest importance for the whole future of Western government.

Gratian himself emphasized with equal vigor both the primacy of the pope and the irrefutable authority of the ancient church councils. Correspondingly, in the Decretist works one finds side by side both strong affirmations of papal sovereignty and a firm adherence to a doctrine of fundamental law. If this is a paradox it is at any rate a perennial one. A tension between the concept of legislative sovereignty and the conviction that a ruler should be in some meaningful sense "under the law" has been characteristic of Western constitutional thought ever since the 12th century.

The Decretists dealt with this problem by seeking in the consensus of the whole Christian community, expressed in the decrees of general councils, norms of faith and order that could be binding on the pope himself. Roman law provided the principle that the *populus,* as well as the emperor, possessed a legislative capacity. But in Roman law itself this led on only to an impracticable doctrine of "dual sovereignty." The Civilian lawyers, when they did not favor outright absolutism, clung to the awkward conception of a legislative authority inhering in the people which could be exercised separately from that of the emperor. The canonists gave a decisive new formulation to this classical doctrine. They suggested that the authority of ruler and community could augment one another so that an act of both together, acting in co-operation, possessed a higher authority than the act of either party alone. In this way the claims for papal sovereignty could be reconciled with the claims for conciliar supremacy, since the canons of a council were by definition acts of an assembly over which the pope presided. They could be regarded as acts of the papal will expressed in its highest and most authoritative form and so as binding on the pope himself considered as a mere individual. Hence in many Decretist works written around 1200 we read that the pope was bound by statutes of councils "touching the faith and the general state of the church." [6]

A common starting-point for canonistic discussions on these questions was Gratian's Dist. 15 c.2, a text of Pope Gregory I which declared that the first four general councils were to be revered "like the four

---

6. *Foundations,* 47-67. Further illustrative texts are published in "Pope and Council: Some New Decretist Texts," 210-212.

Gospels" because their canons were established "by universal consent." This patristic reference to universal consent was important for the canonists since it enabled them to link the authority of general councils with their doctrine that only the whole *congregatio fidelium* was unerring in faith. For the Decretists a general council was not only a meeting of the apostolic college but also a representation of the whole community of the faithful. Bishops were still elected in the 12th century (though the circle of electors had diminished). The bishop represented his people and the canonists turned to the Roman law of proctorship to find a term—*plena potestas*—that could adequately define the authority conferred on a bishop by the very fact of his election (i.e. before his episcopal consecration). Since they wanted general councils to be as fully representative as possible the canonists also argued that others besides bishops could properly be summoned to them. Here they borrowed another phrase from Roman Law, *Quod omnes tangit ab omnibus approbetur.* The words had no constitutional significance in classical law. The canonists turned them into a principle of representative government by arguing that, when matters of faith were to be discussed, representatives of the laity should be invited to general councils since the faith was a matter that "touched" all Christians.[7]

In a famous allocution delieverd to the Roman Rota in 1945 Pope Pius XII argued that democratic structures of authority were utterly incompatible with the form of government established by Christ for His Church. The pope declared that, "in the church as founded by Christ there does not exist and can not exist any . . . judicial power deriving from the people." And he quoted approvingly a phrase from the modern Code, "Those who are admitted to the ecclesiastical hierarchy are not chosen by the community or at the call of the people . . ." It must be emphasized that these modern formulations are quite alien to the spirit of early and medieval Christianity. Against the words of the modern Code we might cite the canonical authority of Pope St. Leo I on the election of bishops, "He who is to preside over all is to be chosen by all."[8] No Catholic will want to deny that a bishop's power comes from God. But it seldom occurred to medieval men to ask whether lawful authority come from God *or* the people. They took it for granted that it came from God *and* the people, that popular consent was the normal way in which the divine will would manifest itself in a Christian community. The canonist Sicardus put the point with force of an epigram, "In these matters God is the bestower;

---

7. *Foundations,* 49 n.1. For a discussion of the whole question see Y. Congar, "quod omnes tangit . . ." *Revue historique de droit francais et etranger* (1958), 210-259.

8. Ep. X, 4 (Migne P.L. 54, 628) cited by Congar, *art. cit.* 225.

we are His instruments." Laurentius Hispanus explained in more detail that, while the papal office was established by God, the individual who was to bear that office had to be designated by human choice.[9]

This distinction between person and office was once more derived from Roman law and again the canonists developed it in an entirely new way. They did this by applying the distinction to the extreme case of a pope who endangered the whole church by becoming a heretic or notorious criminal. The church could not judge the papacy, they agreed. The whole Christian community could not, for example, abolish the papal office, for the office was established by Christ. But, in an extreme emergency, it might be necessary for the community to make a judicial determination that a given individual was not fit to continue in office as pope or had already degraded himself from the papal office by his crimes.[10]

This structure of canonistic ideas exercised a great influence on the theory and practice of secular government during the next two hundred years. In English constitutional law we find emerging a concept of king-in-parliament that was precisely analogous to the canonists idea of pope-and-council. An individual king could be bound by statutes of parliament—although parliament was the king's own court—precisely because parliament expressed the royal will in its more authoritative form. Already by 1300 we find in writs of summons to parliament the terms *plena potestas* and *quod omnes tangit* used in precisely the technical sense that the canonists had first given to them, that is as juridical expressions of the principle of representative government. Also in 1307 the English barons made a sharp distinction between person and office in the political sphere by declaring that their loyalty was owed primarily to the crown rather than to the person of the king and that in defense of the crown they might even take up arms against the king.

Within the church itself, however, the trend was more and more toward unlimited papal absolutism and, during the 14th century, curial theologians and canonists reached unprecedented extremes in their almost frenzied exaltations of papal power. But the earlier canonical tradition was not altogether lost to sight. It was preserved in the *Glossa ordinaria* to Gratian's *Decretum* (which continued to be used as a standard text for the teaching of canon law) and also in the writings of various philosophers

---

9. Sicardus *ad Dist.* 65, MS Augsburg, Stadtbibliothek 1, fol. 89v, "Instrumenta sumus nos, deus collator." For the text of Laurentius see *Foundations,* 56 n.2.
10. *Foundations,* 57-67, "Pope and Council: Some New Decretist Texts," 214-218.

and theologians who, for different reasons, found themselves in opposition to the papacy of Avignon.

This was the situation when the 14th century system of centralized papalism collapsed into the chaos of the Great Schism.

The Council of Constance

The central legislative act of the Council of Constance was the decree *Haec sancta*. We can conveniently consider this decree from three points of view. (1) How did *Haec sancta* come to be enacted? (2) Was it a valid decree? (3) What did it mean?

(1) *How did Haec sancta come to be enacted?* The immediate cause for the enactment of *Haec sancta* was the persistence of the disastrous schism that had broken out in 1378. In that year the cardinals first elected Urban VI as pope in Rome and then repudiated the election on the ground that it had been made under coercion. They then elected a second pope who took up residence in Avignon. After a while it became evident that neither pope could hope to win the allegiance of the whole church. There were then elaborate negotiations aimed at persuading both pontiffs to resign in order to make way for a pope of unity. When these negotiations broke down after years of fruitless bickering a majority of the cardinals from both obediences broke away from their respective popes, and, claiming to represent the Roman church, summoned a general council on their own initiative. This council met at Pisa in 1409. It deposed both the existing popes and elected a third one. Unhappily, instead of ending the schism, this merely produced a third line of popes alongside the other two.

In these same years at the beginning of the fifteenth century there was a great outburst of theoretical writing on the structure of the church by such eminent figures as Gerson, D'Ailly and Zabarella. These authors expounded in systematic treatises on church government all the scattered suggestions of the earlier canonists concerning the due limits of papal authority and the rights of the Christian community.

The second pope of the Pisan line took the title John XXIII. Under intense pressure from the emperor Sigismund he agreed to summon yet another general council to seek a final solution of the schism, and this council duly assembled at Constance toward the end of 1414. It was one of the best attended, most truly representative assemblies in the history of medieval Christendom. John XXIII hoped that the council would merely repeat the condemnation of his two rivals and confirm that John was the true pope. In January and February of 1415, however, it became clear that the council was also determined to proceed against John XXIII himself. (He was indeed a man of notoriously evil life.) On March 21 John fled from the council that he had summoned and threatened to dissolve it.

There followed several days of disorder and dismay at Constance but on March 26 the Fathers of the council gathered their courage John might decree. It became necessary then to enact a conciliar canon and declared that they would stay in session as a general council whatever defining their own authority. *Haec sancta* was first presented to the Fathers for their consideration on March 30. Then came a week of angry debate and intrigue. The cardinals wanted a more moderate decree limited to the immediate emergency situation but their arguments were rejected and on April 6 the council unanimously enacted the following measure:

> This holy synod of Constance, constituting a general council and lawfully assembled to root out the present schism and to bring about the reform of the church in head and members . . . declares that, representing the church militant, it holds its power immediately from Christ and that anyone of whatsoever state or dignity, even if it be papal, is bound to obey it in matters which pertain to the faith, the rooting out of the said schism and the general reform of the church in head and members. Further it declares that any person of whatsoever rank, state or dignity, even if it be the papal, who contumaciously refuses to obey the statutes, mandates, ordinances or instructions made by this holy synod . . . or by any other general council lawfully assembled concerning the aforesaid matters shall be subjected to fitting penance and duly punished . . .[11]

By virtue of the authority asserted in this decree the council deposed John XXIII in May, 1415. Under threat of deposition the Roman pope abdicated in July. The Avignon pope was obdurate to the end and was finally deposed in 1417.

(2) *Was Haec sancta a valid decree?* For four hundred years, from the middle of the 15th century to the middle of the 19th, "Gallican" and "Ultramontane" theologians within the Catholic church wrangled

---

11. *Conciliorum Oecumenicorum Decreta* (Freiburg, 1962), 385.

about the validity of *Haec sancta,* the former group defending the decree, the latter group attacking it. After the defeat of Gallicanism at Vatican Council I it came to be generally assumed among Catholic scholars that *Haec sancta* was invalid and, moreover, that the principle affirmed in it was heretical. In accordance with this pre-supposition an appropriate account of the history of the Great Schism was contrived. It can be found in numerous manuals of church history written for use in Catholic seminaries during the half-century after Vatican Council I.

The account runs like this. The pope validly elected in 1378 was Urban VI of the Roman line and all pontiffs of the Roman line after him were legitimate popes. But only the true pope could summon a general council. The council of Pisa therefore was a mere *conciliabulum.* The pope chosen at Pisa, Alexander V, and his successor, John XXIII, were anti-popes. Accordingly the Council of Constance was not a legitimate council for it was summoned by John XXIII. Its decree *Haec sancta* was therefore not a legitimate decree. *Haec sancta* was also invalid because it attempted to enact into law an unorthodox doctrine concerning the nature of the church that had been first propounded by the condemned heretics, William of Ockham and Marsilius of Padua. Moreover *Haec sancta* was never confirmed by a legitimate pope and so it was invalid for yet a third reason. Finally, the enactment of *Haec sancta* did not bring about the end of the schism. The two "popes" who were deposed in accordance with its terms were both anti-popes. The last true pope of the Roman line voluntarily abdicated and it was this action which left the way open for the election of a pope of unity.

These arguments were essentially circular. On the basis of theological pre-suppositions a structure of historical hypothesis was enacted. These hypotheses were then assumed to be facts and were used to support the underlying presuppositions. Thus the *Lexicon für Theologie und Kirche* (in the edition of 1937) found an example of the workings of divine providence in the fact that only the legitimate pope left the papacy in a legitimate fashion;[12] but this sort of assertion in fact begs the question of who in fact was the legitimate pope.

Several technical monographs published during the 1940's and 1950's undermined the thesis set out above at several crucial points, but the thesis as a whole was not generally attacked by Catholic scholars before the 1960s. The summoning of Vatican Council II stimulated a new

---

12. L.Th. K.9 (1937), 259, cited by Fink, *art. cit. infra* n.14.

interest in ecclesiology among theologians and a new interest in the history of general councils among church historians. Then, rather surprisingly perhaps, the two currents of thought converged in demands for a radical re-evaluation of the Council of Constance that were put forward by numerous scholars including Congar, De Vooght, Fink, Küng, Jedin and Franzen.

In 1960 Paul de Vooght and Yves Congar argued that a decree which was accepted by the whole Catholic world in the years immediately after its enactment as a licit decree of an undoubted general council ought not to be shrugged aside lightly as heretical and invalid.[13] In 1962, Karl August Fink published a brief but devastating attack on the whole "received version" of the history of the Great Schism.[14] Referring to the monographs of Seidlmayer and Prerovsky on the election of 1378,[15] he pointed out that it was quite impossible to affirm, on the basis of strictly historical evidence, that Urban VI was validly elected or that the Roman pontiffs who succeeded him were legitimate popes. The modern historian simply does not know. Nor did men of the early fifteenth century. They were in a state of "invincible ignorance." So are we. The magisterium of the Catholic church has never made a pronouncement on the question. The proceedings of the Council of Pisa, Fink pointed out were not a mere revolutionary expedient but were based on an ancient canonical tradition that permitted the deposition of a pope in certain very exceptional cases.[16] From the point of view of a church historian there seemed no adequate reason to deny that Pisa was a legitimate council and that the popes whose authority was derived from Pisa were legitimate popes.[17]

These arguments were taken up and expanded by Fink's colleague at Tübingen, the theologian Hans Küng. Küng reviewed the

---

13. The essays of De Vooght and Congar were published in *Le Concile et Les Conciles*, ed. B. Botte (Paris, 1960). The most recent statement of De Vooght's position is to be found in his *Les pouvoirs du concile et l'autorite du pape* (Paris, 1965).
14. K. A. Fink, "Zur Beurteilung des grossen abendlandischen Schismas," *Zeitschrift fur Kirchengeschichte*, 73, (1962), 335-343.
15. M. Seidlmayer, *Die Anfange des grossen abendlandischen Schismas* (Münster, 1940): O. Prerovsky, *L'elezione di Urbano VI e L'insorge dello scisma d'occidente* (Rome, 1960).
16. On this tradition see especially H. Zimmermann, "Papstabsetzungen des Mittelalters," *Mitteilungen des Instituts fur Oesterreichische Geschichtsforschung*, 69 (1961), 1-84 and 241-291; 70 (1962), 60-110; 72 (1964), 74-109.
17. The two popes of the Pisan line were called Alexander V and John XXIII. The fact that our own Pope John styled himself John XXIII obviously casts doubts on the legitimacy of his predecessor. On the other hand the next Alexander called himself Alexander VI. As Fink points out there is no consistent Catholic tradition in this matter of nomenclature.

whole history of general councils in the church and suggested that, while the requirements of papal convocation and explicit papal approbation as criteria for the validity of conciliar decrees are indeed insisted on in modern canon law, they are by no means eternal theological verities. Judged by these criteria, not only *Haec sancta,* but also all the canons of the early councils of the church were invalid. Moreover, Küng pointed out, the ideas underlying *Haec sancta* were not derived from the condemned heretics, Ockham and Marsilius, but were based on "the totally orthodox and traditional ecclesiology of the 12th and 13th centuries." (We may add here that several recent monographs on the major conciliar thinkers of the early 15th century have confirmed that all of them rejected the more extreme ideas of Ockham and Marsilius and that all truly believed in the doctrine of papal primacy.[18]) Küng concluded that *Haec sancta* was a vaid decree of a general council and binding on the church for ever.[19]

In 1963, Hubert Jedin, perhaps the most distinguished of German church historians, joined in the discussion. The church is not merely a divine idea, he wrote, but a historical reality, and dogmas about the nature of the church need to be related to the real facts of its history. Given the impossibility of deciding in 1415 which of the rival pontiffs was truly pope, the real facts of the situation were that the schism could be ended only by a decree asserting jurisdiction of the council over all three claimants. To deny the validity of the decree which declared this principle is to deny the validity of the only measure which proved capable of ending the schism.[20]

In opposition to Küng and De Vooght, Jedin maintained that *Haec sancta* was essentially an emergency measure, limited in its validity to the immediate circumstances of the schism. But Jedin also pointed out that the very fact that such a decree could be licitly enacted at all has important implications for the theology of the church. These implications have been considered in a recent article by Helmuth Riedlinger comparing the ecclesiology of Constance with that of Vatican Council I.[21] The decrees

---

18. J. B. Morrall, *Gerson and the Great Schism* (Manchester, 1960): G. Posthumus Meyjes, *Jean Gerson. Zijn Kerkpolitiek en Ecclesiologie* (The Hague, 1963); F. Oakley, *The Political Thought of Pierre d'Ailly* (New Haven, 1964); M. Watanabe, *The Political Ideas of Nicholas of Cusa* (Geneva, 1963); P. Sigmund, *Nicholas of Cusa and Medieval Political Thought* (Cambridge, Mass., 1963).
19. H. Küng, *Structures of the Church* (New York, 1963).
20. H. Jedin, *Bischofliches Konzil oder Kirchenparlament* (Basle, 1963).
21. H. Riedlinger, "Hermeneutische Uberlegungen zu den Konstanzer Dekreten," in A. Franzen and W. Muller (eds), *Das Konzil von Konstanz* (Freiburg, 1964).

Haec sancta and *Pastor aeternus* seem at first sight to be sharply opposed to each other in every possible way. But Riedlinger points out that even dogmatic decrees of general councils have to be expressed in imperfect human language and through the medium of human concepts that are necessarily "time-conditioned." It is possible therefore that two decrees from widely separated centuries may seem verbally opposed to one another and yet each contain a valid sub-stratum of truth. Riedlinger observes that the theologian's task is precisely to distinguish between permanent religious truth and the time-conditioned modes of its expression, and that in order to do this effectively he has to penetrate deeply into the historical context of any particular decree. Theology can only be convincing if it is histori-cally credible, Riedlinger writes. The theologian must accept historical facts as they really were. He cannot just invent history to suit his own theology. If then there is really a convincing historical case for the validity of *Haec sancta* the theologian has to take this into account in his interpretation of the ecclesiology of Vatican Council I. Nevertheless, when all allowances have been made for differences of historical context, Riedlinger thinks that to reconcile the claims of the two councils will be a formidable task. [22]

There the matter rests as far as the theologians are concerned. A historian can only reiterate Jedin's insistence on the historical realities of the early 15th century. The actual historical circumstances of that age convinced Catholics that Christ had not established in His church a simple monarchy in which absolute power was given exclusively to Peter and his successors. Throughout the 14th century the papacy had failed to carry through an urgently needed reform of the church. In the end it had failed even to maintain an external facade of ecclesiastical unity. Christ's promise that his church would never fail had been made good, not by invoking the unfailing powers of Peter, but by appealing to the intrinsic authority of the whole Christian community. These facts never ceased to be true. It became convenient for theologians to forget them.

(3) *What did Haec sancta mean?* The real meaning of *Haec sancta* has not been properly grasped in most modern analyses of the doc-ument and this is a major reason why theologians have found it so hard

22. The conservative arguments against the validity of *Haec sancta* have been restated—unconvincingly it seems to me—by J. Gill, "The Fifth Session of the Council of Constance," *Heythrop Journal*, 5 (1964), 131-143; H. Hurten "Zur Ekklesiologie der Konzilien von Konstanz und Basel," *Theologische Revue*, 59 (1963), 362-371; I. H. Pichler, *Die Verbindlichkeit der Konstanzer Dekrete* (Vienna, 1967). A more balanced criticism is offered by W. Brandmuller in *Romische Quartalschrift*, 62 (1967).

to assimilate the decree into an acceptable framework of Catholic ecclesiology. *Haec sancta* did not—as has usually been assumed—assert that, in normal times when there was a certainly legitimate pope, the sovereign authority of the church resided in a collection of representatives separated from the pope and, if necessary, acting against him. As regards the immediate situation, the Fathers of Constance were claiming authority for themselves at a time when there was no certain pope but only three dubious claimants to the papacy. (In similar fashion the canonists had held that a council could judge a supposed pontiff when his conduct was such as to raise doubts whether he was a true pope or not.) As regards the future, *Haec sancta* declared that all popes were to be bound by the decrees of lawfully assembled general councils in certain defined spheres; but the term "general council" in the normal canonical and theological language of the Middle Ages did not designate as assembly separated from the pope. It meant rather an assembly grouped around the pope as its head. As we have noted, the canonists, on whose works the conciliarists relied so heavily, had often maintained that the pope was bound by the statutes of such councils "touching the faith and the general state of the church." But these same canonists had also sometimes maintained that, in case of a dispute between the pope and all the other bishops of the church, the opinion of the pope was to be preferred.[23] The two propositions were not contradictory. *Haec sancta* affirmed the first one. It took no stand on the second.

The Fathers of Constance intended to enact major decrees of ecclesiastical reform and many of them also intended that a whole series of councils should meet under the presidency of future legitimate pontiffs to enact further necessary reforms. They wanted to guard against the possibility that the whole reform program might be wrecked by the arbitrary will of a single reactionary pontiff. They did not seek to bind future popes to the decisions of general councils in all matters of administrative detail but only to assert the over-riding authority of the council in certain areas where, it seemed to them, the whole future well-being of the church was at stake. If we transpose their claim into modern terms it amounts to an assertion that no future pope can simply abolish the reform decrees of Vatican Council II by an act of arbitrary, individual will. This seems an arguable proposition.

---

23. This was the opinion handed down in the *glossa ordinaria* to the Decretum (*ad* C. 24 q. 1 c. 6). Earlier canonistic opinion on the point was by no means unanimous. See the various views discussed in "Pope and Council; Some New Decretist Texts."

The Aftermath

Medieval conciliarism failed as a viable system of church government for many reasons but, above all, it failed because Pope Eugene IV and his successors were determined that it should fail. When Eugene IV dissolved the Council of Basle before any meaningful work of reform had been accomplished the leaders of the conciliar party were driven to formulate extreme claims against the papacy that really were departures from Catholic tradition. The partisans of the pope on the other hand rejected the moderate conciliarism of Constance as obdurately as they resisted the radicalism of Basle.

At the beginning of the fifteenth century there was a possibility that pope and council, working together in mutual trust, might carry through the desperately needed reform of the church in head and members. In the thirty years after Constance it became evident that the members of the council, isolated from and hostile to the pope, could achieve no significant reform on their own. And the next hundred years showed that the pope alone could not reform the church without the support of a general council. The relapse into papal absolutism after the defeat of the conciliarists was followed—well-nigh inevitably—by the Protestant revolt.

And yet this was not the end of conciliar thought. The very ideas that were rejected in the ecclesiastical polity continued to work like a ferment in the sphere of secular politics. This was pointed out long ago by J. N. Figgis whose views we quoted at the outset. He wrote that, in the works of the great conciliarists, "The theory of a mixed or limited monarchy was set forth in a way which enabled it to become classical" and "Certainly it was so used in later controversies." [24] Figgis made these assertations as intuitive generalizations without full supporting evidence. In the next half century they were never seriously challenged but equally they were never systematically investigated. During the past decade, however, the relationships between 15th century conciliarism and 17th century constitutionalism have been studied in more detail, and it is now quite clear that we are faced with a single developing tradition of constitutional thought and not with mere accidental similarities of doctrine. [25] There are three main lines of influence connecting the conciliarists of the 15th

---

24. *Supra* n. 3.
25. See especially F. Oakley, "On the Road from Constance to 1688," *Journal of British Studies,* 1 (1962), 1-31 and "From Constance to 1688 Revisited," *Journal of the History of Ideas,"* 27 (1966), 429-432.

century with the constitutionalists of the 17th. (1) The English constitutional theorists who preceded Locke were deeply indebted to 16th century French writings against royal absolutism like the *Vindiciae contra tyrannos*. These in turn borrowed extensively from the work of the conciliarists. (2) George Buchanan whose *De iure regni* was one of the most influential works of 16th century political thought was a pupil of John Major — one of the last of the medieval conciliarists — and he was significantly influenced by Major's ideas. (3) Some of the most eminent leaders of the English parliamentary movement of the 17th century — especially William Prynne and Samuel Rutherford — knew at first hand the writings of the conciliarists and made use of their ideas in their own works.

Figgis was thus brilliantly perceptive in sensing a connection between conciliarism and secular constitutionalism. He was, however, quite mistaken in supposing that the interplay between ecclesiastical and secular concepts began only in the years around 1400 and that the conciliarists merely borrowed, and wove into systematic theories, constitutional practices which had already evolved independently in the secular sphere. We have only recently come to understand the canonistic foundations of medieval conciliarism and the full implications of this understanding for the whole history of Western political theory have still to be worked out. It seems clear, at any rate, that in the history of Western constitutionalism the really decisive encounter between secular and ecclesiastical thought was the fusion of the Roman idea of sovereignty with the patristic ideal of a Christian community in the works of the medieval Decretists. The parallel development of parliamentary government in the state and of conciliar theories in the church were both profoundly influenced by the structures of constitutional law formulated by the canonists of the 12th century. The process of interaction between secular and religious thought which produced the constitutional concepts of the modern world has its origins deep in the Middle Ages.

Conclusions

There are two points to be made in conclusion. The first is that Western constitutionalism is not something foreign to the tradition of the Catholic church. If we chose to adopt constitutional forms in the structure of the modern church we should not be borrowing from an alien system. Rather we should be reclaiming a rich part of our own inheritance.

The second point is this. The decrees of Constance were an

attempt to give the church a juridical structure that would be in accordance with its intrinsic collegial nature. In modern times the doctrine of collegiality has been defined for us afresh; but the problem of juridical structure still remains. The Council of Constance failed and the results of that failure were disastrous for the church. We have another chance and we have less excuse for failing. We have not forgotten our history and we are not condemned to repeat it.

V.
GUIDING PRINCIPLES

Authority: Its Source, Nature, and Purpose in the Church

Hamilton Hess

Our aim in this symposium is to discuss the need, the desirability or the possibility of a constitution for the Church. A constitution is a stated body of fundamental principles according to which a society is organized and governed. It defines in practical terms the organizational pattern of the society and specifies the relationships and respective rights and duties of the governors and the governed.

The development of a constitution in any given society presupposes certain definite notions of authority held within that society. Existent notions of authority, of its source, nature and purpose do, in fact, play a large part in determining the shape of a constitution. If it is held by the constitutional framers in a particular society that governing authority derives ultimately from the governed, the governmental structures specified by the constitution will have a strongly representational character. If it is held that governing authority is ultimately derived from the rights of one

Mr. Hamilton Hess teaches in the Graduate Division of the Department of Theology, University of San Francisco. He received his B.A., M.A. (in Theology), and Ph.D. (in Patristics) from Oxford. He was ordained a priest in the American Episcopal Church. Later he entered the Roman Catholic Church. His doctoral dissertation was THE CANONS OF THE COUNCIL OF SARDICA, A.D. 343. A LANDMARK IN THE EARLY DEVELOPMENT OF CANON LAW.

individual or a few, popular participation in governmental activity will be minimal.

In most societies, however, a constitution also finds itself built around certain inherited institutions, and these, as basic ingredients of societal structure, exert a conditioning influence upon the notions of authority which are held. Thus, historically, we find that as well as having a determining influence upon the shape of institutions, notions of authority themselves are partially shaped by institutional climate. A constitution is, then, in the final analysis, the product of a complicated interplay between philosophical and political ideas and pragmatic social institutions.

It is evident that such an interplay is operative within the Church as well as within other societies. We find, in fact, that the cross currents of influence are only the more complicated in the ecclesiastical milieu; for, as a society within a society, both the Church's institutions and the notions of authority which have found expression within her have been influenced by secular institutions and notions, in addition to their bearing the marks of her own unique traditions.

In view of the close interrelation between notions of authority and institutional forms, it is essential that we approach the question of a constitution for the Church with a common understanding of what we mean by ecclesiastical authority. It is the purpose of this paper to provide a perspective treatment of the notion of authority, its source, nature and purpose in the Church. Anything approaching an adequate discussion of this topic is an impossible goal for one short paper, but our aim, again, is simply to suggest perspective approaches to the question of authority which may serve as guidelines, or at least indicate guidelines, for our discussions.

None of us can fail to recognize the fact that the notion of ecclesiastical authority is currently in a state of serious crisis. In its present dimensions, the crisis has arisen largely from three areas of consideration which have had a strongly stimulating effect upon each other. The first is the socio-political climate of twentieth century society. The contemporary Catholic Christian finds it a deeply disturbing fact that the fundamental notions of participated authority, freedom and basic human rights in which he has been nurtured in secular society seem to find only limited expression in the Church. The second factor is the contemporary renewal of biblical and patristic studies, which has revealed the former currency of somewhat different notions and expressions of ecclesiastical authority than those which have been commonly held and utilized within the Catholic Church for a number of centuries past. The third factor is the ecumenical movement. This has had two effects. It has brought Catholics face to face with honest, if not always just and understanding criticism of the notions and expressions of ecclesiastical authority which they have taken for granted, and it has brought forcibly to the Catholic attention the different but frequently authentically Christian notions of authority held by different traditions. Of highest importance among these notions are the directly authoritative claims upon the individual Christian of the Word of God in Scripture and of the Holy Spirit speaking in men's hearts.

As in every crisis, the current reappraisal of the theory and exercise of ecclesiastical authority has its positive and negative aspects. In addition to those who would take a simplistic approach, either by questioning the existence of a truly objective authority within the Church or by postulating a monolithic juridical structure, there are others who foresee the attainment of a balance in theory and in practice which will more closely suit the legitimate demands of the conditions suggested by the three areas of consideration outlined above.

Our probing of the question of a constitution for the Church takes place in the midst of this crisis. It is indeed largely the state of crisis itself and its reappraisal of the notion and exercise of authority within the Church which has brought the constitutional question to the fore. It is essential, however, that we approach our question with the utmost circumspection, for if we believe that we can discern the direction of development which the notion of authority is beginning to take, we can by no means foresee its final expression. For us to fail at this point to take the potential of development into account would lead to a foreshortening of the vision which is needed to promote, constitutionally if necessary, the true liberty under authority of the sons of God.

It may be said with some justification that the Church already has a constitution. It exists as a composite collection of her canon law, conciliar and papal directives and curial judgments. Coming as they do from several different periods of the Church's history, a number of definite notions of ecclesiastical authority are found to be reflected in these many documentary directives regarding the Church's life and structure. And, in accordance with the complexity of influences which we have noted previously, the notions of authority involved are found both to have influenced the shape of the directives and to have been themselves suggested by the conditions which the directives set forth. As well as institutions being formed by a theology of ecclesial operation, we find, parallel to another well known phenomenon, a situation of *lex agendi, lex putandi*.

During the fourth and fifth centuries, for example, the provincial synod became, in the East particularly, the first authoritative organ to operate effectively above the diocesan level for the regulation of everyday affairs of the Church. The form of its operation and the mode of its expression were modelled closely upon the activities of secular provincial government. This was a practical innovation which had very little theological background, but which led to a definitive development of the notion of authority as exercised by the collective episcopate. Beginning at about the same time, and increasingly during the centuries following, the papacy, for very justifiable historical reasons, came to play a practical role in the day to day affairs of the universal Church. Again practice preceded theory, and the hitherto embryonic theology of papal authority underwent a development consequent to the fact of its exercise. We may also note that the classical theological treatises on the Church, which were written from the fourteenth century onward, clearly bear the marks of opposition to Gallicanism, of the controversies over the division of power between Church and state, and the repudiation of the ecclesiological errors of the Protestant Reformation. The notions of authority which these treatises express strongly reflect the understandably dominant, if somewhat one-sided, image of the Church as a coercive, hierarchical structure of divine power.

I am by no means suggesting that we should attempt to sit in judgment upon such developments of fact or theory, or upon the order of their emergence. The dividing lines between human design and providential arrangement are impossible to draw, and human design itself is the stuff with which providential arrangement frequently achieves its ends. My point is that the notions of authority current in any given age are inevitably affected by external circumstance, our own age not excepted, and that we must consciously take this factor into account in discussing the question of authority.

We have become aware of the fact that certain imbalances exist in the Church's structuration, and, in accordance with the factors noted above, it is apparent that these imbalances have either been caused by or are themselves the causes of imbalance in the theology of authority. Upon what criteria do we base these judgments? How, within the living stream of Tradition, are we to say with objective certainty that one attitude represents an imbalance and that another does not? To rest our case upon the fact that the Church's ways seem out of step with those of the modern world, or on the observation that Protestants find the authoritarian atmosphere of the Catholic Church uncongenial, are simply pragmatic and essentially invalid judgments.

We must find better criteria, and these would seem to be the principles by which the legitimate development of doctrine is seen to take place. These principles are based upon the fact of continuity—the unity and identity of an idea with itself through all stages of its development— and upon the realization of original potential. While these criteria have been applied by theologians mainly to doctrines in themselves, they can be and also certainly should be applied to the Church's institutions and modes of operation as either reflecting the doctrines which underly them or as influencing the shape of those doctrines themselves. The unhealthy chasm between dogmatic theology and the visible forms of the Church's life needs to be bridged on all fronts, and fidelity to type and realization of potential in both doctrinal expression and institutional life need continuously to be correlated with each other and to be examined in relation to their origins to ensure balance in development. Considerable progress in this regard has taken place in the area of liturgics and sacramentology, but in the ecclesiological field the process has only just begun.

Even now, however, several imbalances in the area of authority and its institutional expression are evident to us. Without claiming to exhaust the possibilities, and hoping to avoid infringement upon the topic of another paper, we may cite the following: 1) the notion of the prophetic, priestly and kingly powers of Christ being the exclusive possession of the hierarchy, sharable with the faithful by delegation, but without reference to the several ways in which the faithful inherently share in these authoritative functions by virtue of their baptismal commission; 2) the notion of authority as being received by the hierarchy from God for the purpose of ruling over the community from above, rather than as receiving this authority within the context of the community itself for the purpose of ordering the community from within; 3) the frequent operation of authoritative functions in essential separation from the pastoral, liturgical and teaching offices in the church's structure through administrative bureaus on both the diocesan and higher levels; 4) an impersonal legalism in the exercise of authority, resulting both from the preceding and from a top heavy centralization of authority which owes its existence to a long process of the upward absorption of authoritative functions; 5) the notion that because authority is a divine charism, the manner of its exercise is not liable to question nor the competence of its functionaries open to challenge from below; 6) the assumption that, because of the supernatural realities with which it deals, the administration of ecclesiastical authority is not bound to take cognizance of the human situations and basic human rights of its subjects.

These are serious imbalances in the understanding of ecclesiastical authority, and they deeply affect the manner of its exercise. Historically they have arisen from a variety of causes, but theologically they reflect an unbalanced ecclesiology; an ecclesiology which sees the Church more as a structure of spiritual government than as a community of mutual responsibility in the life of the Spirit; an ecclesiology which draws a clear, if only implicit, line of distinction between the "professional Christians" of the governing classes above and the ordinary Christians below; an ecclesiology which emphasizes the juridical powers of the Church's leaders rather than their responsibility to service and witness through the power of the Spirit.

It is clear, of course, that the ecclesiological ailments run more deeply than their structural manifestations. There is need to develop a view of the Church as being herself the sacrament of redemptive activity, as the community of the Spirit, and as the nucleus of a renewed creation. There is a therapeutic need to remember that all images and figures applied to the mystery which is the Church are analogical, and that as a society she is comparable to other societies only to the degree that human institutions can give useful and valid expression to her inner realities. We need to remember also that the several biblical figures and images of the Church, if not all equally profound, are equally valid, needful and complementary. An overemphasis of one to the neglect of another leads to an impoverishment of total understanding. In our own time, for example, Vatican II has given impetus to an enrichment of ecclesiology by its re-emphasis of the Church as the pilgrim People of God, and has given a consequent redress to an over-emphasis of the Church as the earthly Kingdom of God, with all of the connotations of a static and princely authority as characterizing the Church's leadership which such imagery has supported and suggested. The emphasis of ecclesiological images of this nature bear an obvious relation to the notions of authority which we now find to be imbalanced.

Having thus attempted to establish a perspective view of ecclesiastical authority from the standpoint of its notional and situational setting, we turn to a more specific examination of the source, nature and purpose of authority in the Church.

As we have noted, a theology of authority derives from ecclesiology: from a theology of the Church's nature, mission and place in saving history. An adequate and balanced doctrine of authority has its roots in the theology of creation and redemption, for authority is essentially

136

a positive principle of order, which has the perfection of all things, according to their divine purpose, as its end.

In the biblical perspective, man at creation was given authority over all created things in a situation of paradisial perfection. His task as ruler over creation was to perpetuate in order toward its creator the perfections which characterized it. Man's fall destroyed the providential arrangement for harmony and order, placing man himself at disorder with God and his fellow man and with the world around him. The fundamental vision of this profound truth, which appears in the creation stories in the Old Testament, finds its counterpart at various insight levels in Old Testament soteriology in a recurrent vision of the renewal of creation in conditions of paradisial harmony as the end of Yahweh's saving work.

In a consistent pattern of Old Testament thought, God's power is seen to be working through history to this end. The effective principle throughout is the creative, revealing and redemptive will of God, expressed and operative in terms of closely related manifestations of divine power designated as his Word, his Wisdom, and his Spirit, or his Law (Torah). Frequently present is the redeemer-ruler figure, serving as the instrument of divine authority in the fulfillment of history. The Old Testament thus reflects a theology of history which is a soteriology expressing the sovereign authority and saving will of God. We note that throughout the Old Testament God's authority, even when expressed in punitive judgment, is redemptive and perfecting in its purpose and effects. Israel and her institutions are Yahweh's saving instruments, and they are the effective channels of the authority of his Word, his Spirit, his Wisdom and his Law.

The Old Testament soteriology finds its fulfillment in the New. The insights are deepened and a new dimension is added, but the framework remains the same. The communicating, recreative and perfecting Word-Wisdom-Torah are incarnate in Jesus Christ, the fulfillment of the redeemer-ruler figure of Old Testament expectation. The conditions of the paradisial restoration of creation are now supernatural, as man, the head of creation, leads in the process of renewal, both of his own divine similitude and of the perfection of creation, by his participation in the life of the Spirit.

Redemption entails man's being brought into a new relationship with God through a renewal within man himself as he becomes partaker in the renewed humanity of the risen and glorified Christ. Redeemed man is a member of a new order of creation, of which Christ himself is

137

the first-born, and redeemed man lives and moves and breathes in this new order by the power of the Spirit of God. The redeemed order has a societal dimension—a potentially cosmic dimension—as Christ together with his members, as the new Israel, form the anticipatory nucleus of the new heaven and the new earth which is to come.

It is now the New Israel and her institutions which are God's saving instrument and the effective channels of the authority or ordering activity of the Incarnate Word. The institutional Church—invisible in her inner being as the life of the Spirit within the redeemed, but at the same time visible in the tangible operations of that life—is the vehicle and sacrament of our participation in the order of the new creation. The Church is the community of the Holy Spirit, and her life on all levels is characterized by the operations of the Spirit. Thus, the institutional Church is also the sacramentalization of the authority of God as uttered and expressed in his Word.

When we speak of authority in the Church, we mean the authority of the Word of God manifested in Christ the Lord, who rules over his redeemed, ordering them toward their fulfillment in himself. The authority of the Word in the New Israel is a dynamic force which is exercised sacramentally through those within the community who are chosen to perform the ordering functions of teaching, of the supervision of the life of the ecclesial community, of presiding at worship and of the communication of sacramental gifts.

Authority is a function of the Spirit. It is not the possession of the one who exercises it, but is rather the purposeful manner in which he, in the context of his life in the community, is possessed by the Spirit. Authority is in no sense an end in itself, but is an activity of service which has as its end the final ordering and perfection of all creation under the headship of man through the life of the Spirit, the *similitudo dei,* in the Kingdom of God. St. Paul describes the function of authority *(exousia)* as that of building up the community (II Cor 10:8; 13:10), and speaks explicitly of the gifts of the Spirit which make some men apostles, some prophets, some evangelists and some pastors and teachers "for the equipment of the saints for the work of ministry *(diakonia),* for the building up of the body of Christ, until we all attain to . . . mature manhood, to the measure of the stature of the fullness of Christ" (Eph 4:11-13). It is to be noted that it is not simply that those possessing the function of authority are to bring the community to perfection, but that these members are

138

to equip and organize the community to the service of its own attainment of maturity in Christ.

The authoritarian functions within the community are simultaneously and inseparably charismatic and institutional: charismatic as operations of the Holy Spirit within the community, and institutional as being operative through outward, organizational forms. The bishop empowering priests to preside at the Eucharist, the priest granting absolution from sin, a council defining a doctrine to be believed by the people of God, a pope instructing the universal Church on the principles of Christian social doctrine—these are examples of the authoritative institutional charisms, the functions of service and witness for the ordering of the redeemed toward maturity in the renewed humanity of Christ.

It is important for us to bear the fact in mind that historically authority has been exercised in the Church in different ways and through a variety of functional offices. During the first century, the witnessing, organizing and supervisory function of the Twelve and of their apostolic delegates was accompanied on the local scene by various organizational patterns. It seems probable that, at least in the Pauline circle of influence, the headship of the bishop-president, combining in one functional office the "prophetic," "priestly" and "kingly" authoritarian roles, did not emerge until well into the second century. If we are to take Paul's lists of local functionaries seriously (cf. Rom 12:3-8; I Cor 12:28; Eph 4:7-12), we are to assume that doctrinal teachers, governors, pastors and eucharistic presidents were frequently different persons within the same community. If nothing else, these facts suggest that it has been external and practical considerations rather than an inherent necessity of structure which has subsequently tied the exercise of authority to a very few offices which are related through a chain of command.

An examination of the Church's understanding and exercise of her authority during the first three centuries clearly indicates two bases or operational media of authority. These are the dominically instituted apostolate on the one hand and the corporate body of the Christian community on the other. The witnessing, organizing and supervisory functions of the apostolate find their continuance in the local episcopate and in the universal apostolate of the successors of Peter. The authoritative functions of the Christian community are derived from the priestly, royal and prophetic character of the people of the New Israel, and they are expressed both corporately and representationally on behalf of the community by chosen members.

The prerogative of authoritative, corporate action by the community as a whole is frequently reflected in the New Testament. A few examples will suffice: the community itself chooses those who are set apart for service within it (Acts 6:2-5); it sends forth Apostles and messengers (Acts 11:22; 15:22); it "tests" the teachings of prophets (I Thess 5:20-21); it admits to or excludes from its own fellowship those who are judged worthy or unworthy (I Cor 5:4; II John 10).

Contrary to presuppositions engendered by the later history of the presbyteral office, the representational expression of the authority of the local Christian community in the conduct of its own affairs is seen preeminently expressed in the presbyterate of the first to third centuries. Although various influences were at work in the shaping of the structures of the New Israel, the organizational pattern of the local Christian community seems to have been most strongly influenced by that of the Jewish synagogal congregation. The governing officials of the synagogue were elders: men of "lay" status—that is, non-rabbinic and non-priestly—who were respected members of the community and elected for life by the community itself.

In the local Christian congregation also, we find the "elders" (*presbyteroi*) as a representational body selected from among the members of the community and corporately exercising oversight in matters of discipline, teaching and in questions of general community concern. During the first century their oversight was exercised either by themselves as an autonomous group under apostolic supervision, as in the Pauline circle, or in cooperation with a local individual figure of recognized leadership, such as James of the Jerusalem church. While Paul himself nowhere mentions the presbyterate by name, it is clear in his writings that *episcope* (the function of oversight) is corporately exercised in the churches of his foundation, and that those who exercise it are equivalent to the presbyters mentioned elsewhere in the New Testament. In Acts 14:23 Luke tells of Paul's appointment of presbyters in every church, and those to whom Paul refers as *episcopoi* in his speech at Miletus (Acts 20:28) are also described by the Lukan narrative as *presbyteroi* (Acts 20:17). In I Peter 5:1, corporate presbyteral responsibility for the affairs of the communities addressed is assumed, and the same is reflected in James 5:14. It seems probable that the Johannine sphere of influence in Asia Minor witnesses to the relatively early development of the "monarchial" episcopate (see, for example, the implied leadership status of Diotrophes in III John), but here also the presbyterate is found as a corporate organ sharing in the governmental functions (see the numerous references to the presbyterate in the Johannine Apocalypse).

The local church of the second century was characterized by a universally emerging organizational pattern in which the collegial presbyterate exercised its governmental and teaching function within the community under the presidency of one who alone bore the title of "bishop," and to whom alone pastoral and liturgical functions properly appertained. It is central to our point to note that the presbyterate of this early period was essentially what we would call a representative, "lay" governing body. In numerous documents we find the presbyters referred to as the "counsellors" or "assessors" of the bishop, and a qualification of maturity in years appertained to the presbyterate as a guarantee of responsible standing as an "elder" of the community, whereas no such qualification attached to the episcopate. The presbyterate had no liturgical nor pastoral function as such. The eucharistic presidency and pastoral functions in the Pauline circle before the introduction of the liturgical-pastoral episcopate were evidently exercised by certain members of the presbyteral body (Paul refers specifically to "presidents" and "pastors"—Romans 12:8 and Eph 4:11), but presidency and pastoral functions universally became the proper functions of the bishop-president as that office emerged within the young Christian communities. It is only later, in the third century, that the presbyterate gained a properly liturgical and pastoral function as its members regularly began to serve as delegated substitutes for the bishop in the Christian congregations which were rapidly multiplying around the mother churches.

This view of the presbyteral office is given complete support by the evidence available to us. The specific functions which we find the presbyteral body fulfilling within the community are those of disciplinary oversight, general administration of community affairs, and a responsibility for purity of doctrine. It is noteworthy that until the third century, when evidence for concelebration is first seen in the *Apostolic Tradition* of Hippolytus of Rome, the presbyteral body had a place of honor at the Eucharist, but no ministerial function. This is clearly reflected in such disparate sources as the letter of Clement of Rome to the Corinthians (40.5) and the Syriac *Didascalia* (ch. 19). The place and function of the presbyterate in the community is well illustrated by the ordination prayers which have come down to us from the patristic period. The earlier presbyteral ordination prayers, as contained in Hippolytus' *Apostolic Tradition* and in the "Prayer Book" of Serapion of Thmuis in Egypt, give reference solely to administrative, disciplinary and teaching functions. Presbyteral ordination

141

prayers deriving from the late fourth century and beyond, ascribe a sacerdotal function to the presbyterate, which, as we have noted, was increasingly exercised by delegation from the bishop-president of the local community from the third century onward, and gradually became normal to an altered presbyteral office.

This transformation of the presbyteral office from its original function as an expression by representation of the corporate authority of the community itself to an extension of the pastoral and liturgical office of the episcopate clearly left a functional vacuum within the community. It was apparently as a short-lived attempt to fill this vacuum that we find the *seniores ecclesiastici*, mentioned by Tertullian and others, as quasi-official lay leaders within the local community in the African Church of the third century.

At the same time there also existed strictly corporate authoritarian functions which were performed by the pre-Nicene community. The Church during this period was consciously identified with its general membership, the royal priesthood, the chosen race, the holy nation of I Peter 2:9. The people surrounded the bishop and presbyters as co-offerers of the Eucharistic gifts, as co-sanctifiers of the world, and as cooperators in the administration of the Church's affairs. St. Cyprian tells us that he made it a rule of his episcopal ministry to do "nothing without the advice of the presbyters and the consent of the laity" (Epistle lxvii.3). One of the most important functions of corporate authority was the popular election of bishops, which persisted until the fourth century in the East and even later in the West. Cyprian again writes that the laity "ought to separate themselves from a sinful prelate [*praepositus*=head of a Christian community] and not associate themselves with the sacrifices of a sacreligious priest [*sacerdos*=bishop], especially since they themselves have the power either to choose worthy priests or to reject unworthy ones" *(ibid.).* The forceful attribution of these prerogatives is startling to the later Catholic ear, but their statement is no exaggeration of the claims to authority asserted by the local Christian community during the pre-Nicene period. As another example, Polycarp, in his Epistle to the Philippians (11), exhorts the community at Philippi to restore to communion as "frail and erring members" a fallen former presbyter and his wife, thus indicating the existence of a recognized power of corporate sanction within the community.

The fact that the history of Christian institutions records a gradual shrivelling and ultimately virtual disappearance of the authoritarian functions of the community itself, both corporately and representationally

142

exercised, does not negate the essential existence of a base of ecclesiastical authority within the community which gives legitimate expression by the power of the Spirit to the divine will and judgment. We might observe in passing that the relatively recent attention paid to the *consensus fidelium* in questions of doctrine is a renewal of one aspect of the theology of corporate authority. Also, the recent inclusion of laymen in newly created diocesan advisory commissions is a definite step toward the renewal of the expression of the corporate authoritative judgment by representation.

The two bases of authority which we have noted are, of course, two modes of the expression of *one authority*—the authority of the Word of God—exercised within the Church. The bases are wholly complementary, and at several points their functions coalesce. The integral relationship of the bases as authoritative modes *within* and *for* the community is to be emphasized. The apostolic functionaries themselves are members of the community, sharing in all respects in its life, privileges and obligations, and chosen by the community for the ordering of its own life in the Spirit and the activities of its redemptive mission. While the autonomous operation of the apostolic base of authority is possible, and has, in fact, been for many centuries in virtually sole operation in practice, this authoritative function from above stands in need of its complementary authoritative function from below. For apostolic authority to suppress the functioning of the corporate communitarian authority is to create a condition inevitably leading to serious imbalances in the exercise and in the theology of ecclesiastical authority in general.

The theological and practical needs in the area of authority in our own age of renewal are, it is suggested, a view and exercise of authority as service for witness and for the ordering of the redeemed toward their own redemptive function and final end through the complementary operation of the two authoritative bases within the Christian Community. These, in their realization, will necessarily entail a decentralization in the exercise of authority, already in fact begun, which will enable its effective expression through the organs in which it properly resides on the local and diocesan as well as the universal levels.

By no means are we suggesting the introduction of structural expressions of ecclesiastical authority which are to be seen as parallel or rival to those of the Apostolic base. We re-emphasize the complementary nature of the communitarian base and stress that its existence and orientation are provided solely by the Apostolic functions of leadership and of the sacramental conferring of charisms upon the community itself by the papal and episcopal offices. Under these given theological conditions of the relationship between the Apostolic and communitarian bases of authority, competition or rivalry can hardly be seen to exist. Tensions and stresses may well arise, as indeed they are seen to exist today between these self-same poles within the Church, but the dialectic of tension and stress, if properly regarded and fearlessly treated as a dynamic and creative element within the life of the Church, is a needed factor for vitality, for growth and for the continual adaptation of the Church's ways to correspond to the needs and mentality of men in every age.

A SELECT BIBLIOGRAPHY

Jean Colson, *Les fonctions ecclésiales aux deux premiers siècles,* Desclée de Brouwer, Paris, 1956

John L. McKenzie, S.J., *Authority in the Church,* Sheed and Ward, New York, 1966

Joseph M. Powers, "The Layman in the Church," in *Current Trends in Theology* (edited by D.J. Wolf, S.J. and J.V. Schall, S.J.), Doubleday and Co., Garden City, New York, 1965

John M. Todd (ed.), *Problems of Authority,* Helicon Press, Baltimore, 1962

Freedom, Authority, Community

John Courtney Murray, S. J.

Some people today speak of a "crisis of authority" in the Church; others speak of a "crisis of freedom." For my own part, I should prefer to speak of a "crisis of community." The reasons for this description of the situation will appear, I hope, in what follows.

Vatican Council II did not create the crisis; its roots are deep in the past. But the Council brought the crisis into the open. In the first place, the Declaration on Religious Freedom (*Dignitatis Humanae*) said, in effect, that in political society the human person is to live his relation with God, or even with his private idol, in freedom — within a zone of freedom juridically guaranteed against invasion by any form of coercion. This proposition, the Council added, is the product of a biblical insight, though centuries of secular and religious experience were needed in order to bring it to explicit conceptualization.

In the second place, the Constitution on the Church in the Modern World (*Gaudium et Spes*) affirmed, in effect, that the relation of

Father John Courtney Murray, S.J., was for many years a professor of Dogmatic The-ology at Woodstock College. He died on August 16, 1967, in New York City. Often consulted on matters of national policy, one of his works was WE HOLD THESE TRUTHS on the dynamic of Church and State in the American experience. He was one of the chief architects of the Vatican II "Declaration on Religious Liberty."

the Church to the world and of the world to the Church is to be lived in freedom. Freedom, Paul VI said in his momentous address to statesmen on Dec. 8, 1965, is all that the Church asks of the political world — freedom for its apostolic ministry, freedom for the Christian life, freedom for spiritual and peaceful entrance into the political world, there to make moral judgments when political affairs raise moral issues. In turn, the constitution generously acknowledged that the world too has its rightful freedom to live its own life — or rather, its many lives: political, economic, social, cultural, scientific — in accordance with autonomous dynamisms and structures. These respective claims of freedom, the Council implied, are likewise rooted in a biblical insight—that the Church is of God, and so too, though in a different way, is the world.

Having laid down these propositions bearing on freedom, the Council inevitably raised the next question, concerning freedom in the Church. Is not the Christian life within the Christian community to be lived in freedom? Even the essential Christian experience of obedience to the authority of the Church — is it not somehow to be an experience of Christian freedom in the evangelical sense? This is the question, not directly touched by the Council, which now commands serious theological consideration in the light of the doctrine of the Council and of its spirit— indeed, in the light of the Council itself as a splendid "event of freedom" in the ongoing life of the Church.

1 / Classical Conception From a historical point of view, the need for new reflection on the relation between authority and freedom in the Church derives from the fact that presently this relation exhibits an imbalance. In order to grasp this fact, it will be sufficient for the moment to go back only as far as Leo XIII and to consider three aspects of his thought.

First, there is his retrospective reading of history, visible, for instance, in the famous "Once upon a time" paragraph (*Fuit aliquando tempus*) in *Immortale Dei*. Once upon a time there was a Golden Age, the medieval period. It was the age of Christian unity, of the alliance of the Two Powers, of the obedience of both princes and peoples to the authority of the Church. Then came the Reformation. Essentially it was a revolt against the authority of the Church, and in reaction to it the Church laid heavy, almost exclusive emphasis, on its own authority. Later, by a sequence that was not only historical but also logical, there came the

146

Revolution. It was essentially a revolt against the authority of God Himself, launched by the revolutionary slogan: "No one stands above man" (*homini antistare nemimem*). Again in polemic reaction, the Church rallied to the defense of the sovereignty of God, of the "rights of God," of the doctrine that there is no true freedom except under the law of God.

Both of these reactions were historically inevitable and doctrinally justifiable. The Church fashions its doctrine under the signs of the times, and the Reformation and the Revolution were then the signs of the times. But the doctrine formed under them could not but exhibit a certain hypertrophy of the principle of authority, and a corresponding atrophy of the principle of freedom.

In the second place, there is Leo XIII's conception of the political relationship between ruler and ruled in civil society. It is a simple vertical relationship within which the ruled are merely subjects, whose single duty is obedience to authority. Only in the most inchoative fashion does one find in Leo the notion of the "citizen," who is equipped with political and civil rights and protected in their exercise. His emphasis falls on political authority, which is invested with a certain majesty as being from God, and which is to be exercised in paternal fashion in imitation of the divine sovereignty. In turn, the submission of the subject is to exhibit a certain filial quality. Moreover, society itself is to be built, as it were, from the top down. The "prince" is the primary bearer and agent of the social process. *Qualis rex, talis grex*. The ruler is to be the tutor and guardian of virtue in the body politic; the whole of the common good is committed to his charge. The people are simply the object of rule. Leo XIII's political doctrine was plainly authoritarian. It was fashioned under the political signs of the times — the laicist conception of the state and the Jacobin conception of the sovereignty of the people. In that moment in the history of continental Europe, Leo could not assume the patronage of political freedom.

In the third place, there is Leo XIII's ecclesiology, as summed up, for instance, in the encyclical *Satis Cognitum* (1896) in which he says: "We have faithfully depicted the image and figure (*imaginem atque formam*) of the Church as divinely established." The encyclical is, in effect, a lengthy, profound, magisterial commentary on the Vatican I constitution *Pastor Aeternus*, which was the splendid sign of the theological times. The portrait of the Church that emerges is really a portrait of the role of the apostolic office, and in particular the Petrine office, in the Church. In consequence, the ecclesial relationship — to call it such, on the analogy of the political relationship — is the simple vertical relationship between ruler and ruled. The function of the faithful appears simply as obedience to the doctrinal and jurisdictional authority of the Church.

It was within these perspectives that the classical doctrine on the relation of freedom and authority in the Church was fashioned. Those who hold office make the decisions, doctrinal and pastoral. The faithful in the ranks submit to the decisions and execute the orders. The concept of obedience is likewise simple. To obey is to do the will of the superior; that is the essence of obedience. And the perfection of obedience is to make the will of the superior one's own will. In both instances the motive is the vision of God in the superior, who is the mediator of the divine will and the agent of divine providence in regard of his subjects, in such wise that union with his will means union with the will of God. The further motive, to be adduced when obedience means self-sacrifice, is the vision of Christ, who made Himself obedient even unto death.

II / New Signs of the Times

The trouble is that this classical concept of the ecclesial relationship is today experienced as being true indeed, but not the whole truth —as being good indeed, but not good enough to meet the needs of the moment. The signs of the times are new. The age of anti-Reform polemic has gone over into the age of ecumenism. The will of the Church to break with the world of Revolution has given way to a new will to effect that "compenetration" between the Church of today and the world of today in which *Gaudium et Spes* has spoken. The perspectives in which history is now viewed open out not from a supposed Golden Age in the past (whose luster is now seen to be dulled with the tarnish of much immaturity), but from the present moment. They are set not by nostalgia for the past, visible even in Leo XIII's *Satis Cognitum,* but by the solid doctrine of the eschatological character of the Christian existence, which requires it to look resolutely to the future— to the coming-to-be of the Kingdom.

New signs of the times have become visible and were fully recognized at Vatican Council II. The first is man's growing consciousness of his dignity as a person, which requires that he act on his own responsibility and therefore in freedom. The second is man's growing consciousness of community, of that being with the others and for the others which is revealed, for instance, in the phenomenon of "socialization" in the sense of *Mater et Magistra.* The Church in Council assembled clearly assumed the patronage — though in no patronizing sense — of these two related on-going movements in the growth of human consciousness. The Council further undertook the renewal and reform of Christian doctrine and life in the light of these new signs of the times. In particular, the times demand a reconsideration of the classical concept of the ecclesial relationship — a new development, doctrinal and practical, in the relation between authority and freedom in the Church.

The difficulty with the classical conception, as experienced at the moment, is clear enough. It is sometimes stated by saying that obedience is a bar to the self-fulfillment of the individual. The statement may contain a fallacy — an individualistic concept of self-fulfillment, and a failure to realize that self-fulfillment is not simply an affair of freedom but also an affair of community. Briefly, self-fulfillment is the achievement of freedom for communion with the others. Therefore it is also somehow an affair of obedience to authority; for in every kind of community there is always some kind of authority.

The fallacy aside, it must be said that the contemporary difficulty with the classical conception is rooted in a truth — in an experience of the truth that the signs of the times reveal. What is really being said is that sheer submission to the will of the superior and mere execution of his orders do not satisfy the exigencies of the dignity of the person. They do not call into play the freedom of the person at its deepest point, where freedom appears as love. Still less do they exhaust the responsibilities of the person, which are to participate fully in community, and to contribute actively to community. Thus stated, the contemporary difficulty is seen to be entirely valid. It is not to be solved by methods of repression of the principle of authority: that authority is to be obeyed simply because it is authority.

III / In the Service of the Community

There is a need, therefore, to view the issue of freedom and authority in the new perspectives created by the signs of the times—that is, to view the issue within the context of community, which is the milieu wherein the dignity of the person is realized. Community is the context both of command and of obedience. Community is also the finality both of command and obedience. Authority is indeed from God, but it is exercised in community over human persons. The freedom of the human person is also from God, and it is to be used in community for the benefit of the others.

149

Moreover, since both authority and freedom stand in the service of the community, they must be related not only vertically but also horizontally, as we shall see.

1. THE CHURCH, A UNIQUE COMMUNITY

It may be well to remark here that there is no univocal definition of the ruler-ruled relationship because there is no univocal definition of community. This latter term is analogous. The realities it designates — the family, political society, voluntary associations, the Church are somewhat the same and entirely different, one from another. In the case of the Church, which is at once a family and a society and a form of voluntary association, the essential thing is to attend to the *maior dissimilitudo*. Within the uniqueness of the Church as a community, the uniqueness of the relation of Christian freedom to ecclesiastical authority comes to view. Happily, Vatican Council II, which raised the issue of freedom and authority in the Church, also created the perspectives within which its resolution becomes newly possible. Four aspects of conciliar ecclesiology are pertinent here.

a. The Church Is the People of God

In the first place, the Constitution on the Church (*Lumen Gentium*) presents the Church in the first instance as the People of God. The first characteristic of the People is that it "has for its condition the dignity and the freedom of the children of God, in whose hearts the Holy Spirit dwells as in a temple." The basic condition of the People is therefore one of equality in dignity and freedom, established by the common possession of the Spirit. A consequent characteristic of the People is its charismatic quality as a prophetic, royal and priestly People. The Spirit "distributes special graces among the faithful of every rank, and by these gifts he makes them able and ready to undertake the various tasks and offices useful for the renewal and upbuilding of the Church, according to the Apostle: 'To each is given the manifestation of the Spirit for the common good' (1 Cor. 12-7)." In particular, as the Constitution on Divine Revelation (*Dei Verbum*) says, God through the Spirit "uninterruptibly converses with the Bride of his beloved Son," and the Spirit continually "leads unto all truth those who believe and makes the word of Christ dwell abundantly in them." The dignity of the People and its common endowment of Christian freedom importantly consists in the charismatic quality of its members.

150

b. The Church Is a Communion

In the second place, the Council presents the Church as a communion *(koinonia)*. Its infinite inner form is the Holy Spirit Himself, the subsistent love of Father and Son, who is the presence of God in the midst of His People. In consequence, the Church is in the first instance an interpersonal community, whose members are united in love of the Father through Christ and in the Spirit, and also united with one another by the Spirit of Christ, through whom they have access not only to the Father but to one another. The consequence here is one of immense importance, namely, that as an interpersonal community the Church is an end in itself, an ultimate reality, as eschatological reality in a temporal realization thereof. As a communion *sui generis*, the Church has for its primary purpose simply to be a communion. At such it will endure beyond time, forever, in what is called the communion of saints.

c. The Church Is a Witness to the World

In the third place, precisely as an interpersonal communion of love, the Church has a service *(diakonia)* to perform toward all humanity. That is to say, the divine love that is the form of the People, in witness *(martyrion)*, to draw all men into the communion of love, so that they may participate in the response of faith and love to the love whereby the Father loves His own People, purchased by the blood of His Son. In other words, precisely as an interpersonal community *sui generis*, the Church is also a functional community, that is, a community with a work to do, an action to perform — the action of God in history, which is to "gather into one the children of God who are scattered abroad" (John 11:52). Moreover, the work of the community, which is a work of love, is not extrinsic to the thematic of the community; it is woven, as it were, into this thematic as an essential element of it. That is to say, the interpersonal community, united in love, is also united by the missionary work of love to which it is called by its very nature.

Regarded as a functional community, however, the Church is not an end in itself but a means to a higher end — its own growing self-realization and perfection as an interpersonal community. There will come a day when the Messianic function of the Church will have been finished— the Day of the Lord, when the gathering of the People will be complete and the reign of Christ definitively established: "Then comes the end, when he delivers the kingdom to God the Father" (1 Cor. 15:24).

d. The Church Is a Visible Society

In the fourth place, the Church is not only a community of

faith and love but also a visible society; it therefore exhibits a structure of authority and a juridical order. Moreover, the Church is an organized society precisely as a community of faith and love with a function to perform in history. The societal aspect of the Church is not alien or extrinsic to its communal and functional aspects, but essential to both of them and inherent in each of them. That is to say, the organization of the society is required by the purposes of the community, both for the sake of its own unity as an interpersonal communion and also for the sake of its action in history. The hierarchically ordered society — its structure of authority and its juridical order — stands in the service of the community, to assist in perfecting its unity and in performing its function.

The structure of authority in the Church is unique, as the community it structures is likewise unique. It is both doctrinal and jurisdictional — a power of authoritative teaching and of imperative rule. Moreover, the structure is not merely a matter of political and sociological necessity, as in the case of the civil community. This latter is simply a functional community, which is therefore organized only in order to get its work done—its work being what is called the common good. Here the *maior dissimilitudo* appears. The Church is organized as a society *sui generis*, an interpersonal, eschatological communion of faith and love and a historical, missionary community whose work in history expresses its own inner reality.

2. FUNCTIONS OF AUTHORITY IN THE CHURCH

These four themes in the ecclesiology of Vatican II are, of course, entirely traditional. The order of their arrangement, however, is distinctive; so too is the weight of emphasis distributed among them. For Leo XIII, for instance, the Church was both community and society, indissolubly; so it is presented in *Satis Cognitum*. But the weight of his emphasis falls heavily on the societal aspect and on the structure of authority in the Church. It may be fairly, if rather broadly, said that Leo XIII comes to the notion of the Church as community through the notion of the Church as society. And in his construction, the functions of Christian freedom are not readily apparent; they are, in fact, obscured. Authority seems, as it were, to stand over the community as a power to decide and command. In contrast, Vatican II comes to the notion of the Church as society through the notion of the Church as community. Authority therefore stands, as it were, within the community, as a ministry to be performed in the service of the community. Within the perspectives created by this newly accented construction of traditional doctrine, the ecclesial relationship can be more adequately understood and therefore stated with a new nicety of balance. In particular, the functions of Christian freedom emerge into new clarity, in themselves and in their relation to the correspondent functions of authority. The new clarity radiates from the notion of the Church as community, now made newly luminous.

The functions of authority appear to be three, in hierarchical order. And each of them is a function of service to the community.

a. Unitive Function

The first function is unitive. Authority is to be and do what God Himself, through Christ and in the Spirit, is and does. He gathers, unites, establishes communion. This too is the primary function of authority. Moreover, God gathers His Church by initiating and sustaining with men the "dialogue of salvation," brilliantly described by Paul VI in *Ecclesiam Suam*. God communicates with His People, eliciting from them the response of faith and love. His call to them is an imperative laid upon them, but it is, in the words of Paul VI, a "demand of love" (*domanda di amore*), to which the response must be free. So, too, authority performs its unitive function through dialogue with the charismatic body of the faithful. The purpose of the ecclesiastical dialogue, as of the divine dialogue, is to build and strengthen the community; to guide it, under the guidance of the Spirit, toward the full truth. About what? About itself, in the first instance. The dialogue is to deepen that "self-awareness" on the part of the community which was a major theme, and also a major achievement, of Vatican II.

Authority therefore elicits from the charismatic community of Christian faith the insights of each into the faith, for the enlightment of all. (This function receives new emphasis in the new charter of the reformed Congregation on the Doctrine of Faith; it was also strongly advanced in the discourse of Paul VI on Oct. 1, 1966, to the International Congress on the Theology of Vatican Council II, when he spoke of the reciprocal dependency of the magistery upon the theologian and of the theologian upon the magistery.) Moreover, authority stirs the love of the charismatic members of the community for the community to be shown in service of the community. Finally, authority solicits the informed concern of the community for the work of the community — its relations with the world, its mission of salvation and its spiritual mission in the temporal order. (This function is broadly emphasized all through the Constitution on the Church in the Modern World, as well as in almost all the other conciliar documents.)

153

The primacy of this unitive function of authority, to be discharged through dialogue, results from the primacy of the notion of the Church as an interpersonal community whose conscious unity is an end in itself. This primary dialogic function also depends for its performance on the reality of the People of God as a charismatic body, whose basic condition is one of equality in Christian dignity and freedom. It follows therefore that the unitive function of authority is to be carried out under respect for this basic condition. *Lumen Gentium* is careful to provide room in the Church for all manner of legitimate diversities and pluralisms — in rites, theologies, spiritualities, apostolates, etc. — which, so far from damaging the unity of the community, constitute an enrichment of it. The principle of the Declaration on Religious Freedom — that there should be in society as much freedom as possible and only as much restriction as necessary — applies analogously in the Church. Only "in necessary things" is unity itself necessary.

It may be remarked here that the modes and manners in which authority is to perform its unitive function through dialogue are still problematical today, in this area of *assestamento* (adjustment). New structures of communication need to be created (for instance, the Synod that will meet in 1967). Older structures need reformation, as in the case of the Roman dicasteries. Experiments are called for that will yield the necessary experience. The problem is not simply to conceptualize in theological terms the relation between authority and freedom in the Christian community, as it appears in new perspectives; this relation must be lived, in all concreteness and practicality. Thus the experience of life will give vitality to the theology.

b. Decisive or Directive Function

The second function of authority may be called decisive or directive. It hardly needs lengthy description, since it already is a familiar thing, prominent perhaps to the point of undue emphasis in the classical conception of an older day. The decisive function is necessary because the Church is a community of faith, and it was to the magistery that the guardianship of the deposit of the faith was committed. The directive function is needed because the Church is a functional community organized for action in history. It is to be noted, however, that the necessity of the function is not merely a matter of efficiency, to insure that the work of the Church gets done. The necessity is grounded in the very nature of the community. The point is to insure that the work done is the work of the Church which it is when it is done under direction. The even more important point is to insure that the Body acts as one in the action of its members, singly and collectively.

Thus the decisive and directive function of authority is in a true sense a modality of its unitive function. Moreover, the performance of this secondary function supposes that the primary function has already been performed; that the dialogue, whether doctrinal or pastoral, has been afoot between the community and its teachers and pastors; that therefore the decisions and directives, without ceasing to derive their force from apostolic authority, are also the decisions and directives of the community, whose common good they serve.

c. Corrective or Punitive Function

The third function of authority is corrective or punitive. It is an accidental function, in the sense that it is necessary only because the People of God, on its pilgrim way through history is a sinful People. It is also a function of service to the community, which needs to be protected against the egoisms — whether of thought or of action — that would destroy its unity or damage its work. Again, therefore, this function of correction appears as a modality of the unitive function of authority. What comes to the fore today is the need that the corrective or punitive function of authority should be performed under regard for what is called, in the common-law tradition, "due process." The demand for due process of law is an exigence of Christian dignity and freedom. It is to be satisfied as exactly in the Church as in civil society (one might indeed say, more exactly.)

3. FUNCTIONS OF CHRISTIAN FREEDOM IN THE CHURCH

Three functions of Christian freedom in the Church correspond to the three functions of ecclesiastical authority. They are likewise functions of service to the community.

a. Charismatic Function

The primary function may be called, for the sake of a name, charismatic. It is the free response of the community and of all its members to the unitive function of authority, whose initial act is the invitation to dialogue (on which the Council more than once laid emphasis). The Spirit is given to the Christian not only for his own sanctification and enjoyment, but also for the growth of the community in conscious self-awareness and for the fuller development of its action in history. Concretely, the commu-

155

nity uses the gift of the Spirit by sustaining its part in the dialogue with authority, in that confidence of utterance that reveals — in our times, as in those of the Acts of the Apostles — the presence of the Spirit.

The primary function of Christian freedom corresponds therefore to the nature of freedom in its most profound sense — to the nature of freedom as love, as the capacity for self-communication, as the spontaneous impulse to minister and not be ministered to, as the outgoing will to communion with the others. "For you were called to freedom, brethren," St. Paul proclaims (Gal. 5:13). Whatever else the call may imply, it is a call to love: ". . . . . . through love to be servants of one another" (*loc. cit.*). The forms of service within the community are manifold, but the primary service to the community is to participate in the dialogue of salvation that is continually going on in the community. This participation is the first exercise of Christian freedom. It is also an exercise in obedience, in the horizontal dimension that obedience assumes when it is situated, with authority, within community, and therefore in dialogic relation to authority, united to authority in a ministry of love toward the community.

b. Executive Function

The second function of Christian freedom may be called, again for the sake of a name, executive. It corresponds to the decisive and directive functions of authority. It also corresponds to the formal notion of freedom as duty — the freedom whereby one does what one ought to do. Here, of course, obedience may occasionally appear as self-sacrifice. The act of obedience is not, of course, *per se* an act of sacrifice; it is simply an act of Christian freedom. Obedience assumes a sacrificial quality only when Christian freedom meets the resistance of what Paul calls "the flesh." And the premise of obedience as sacrifice is always the profound nature of freedom as love — the love whereby one freely engages oneself in the paschal mystery. Hence obedience, as an act of Christian freedom, even when it is sacrificial — especially when it is sacrificial — is always the act of self-fulfillment. It is the expression of one's self-awareness that one is called to be in the image of the Son Incarnate, who freely gave His life for the many and thus "went His way" to the self-fulfillment that was His resurrection. Finally, whether sacrificial or not, the executive function of Christian freedom, which consists in acceptance of the decisions and directives of authority, is always performed within the community, in and for which He works. Therefore this secondary function of freedom is related to the primary function, the charismatic function of love whereby I contribute to dialogue to the unity of the communion that is the Church. The

156

dialogue is not an end in itself; it looks towards decisions and directives. In their issuance and acceptance, the community comes together in a new way.

c. Self-corrective Function

The third function of Christian freedom may have to go without a name, unless one calls it self-corrective, in order to mark its correspondence to the corrective function of authority. It is the free act of Christian refusal to "submit again to a yoke of slavery" (Gal. 5:1). More broadly, it is the Christian rejection of the temptation, inherent in the psychological notion of freedom as choice, to "use your freedom as an opportunity for the flesh" (Gal. 5:13). One might call it the "mortifying" act of Christian freedom; the word may not be popular today, but the notion is still Pauline (cf. Rom. 8:13). In any event, it is the act whereby Christian freedom stands forth in all its evangelical newness, unique among all the modalities of freedom that men have claimed or hoped for or dreamed of. "It was that we might be free" in this new way, says St. Paul, "that Christ has freed us" (Gal. 5:1).

CONCLUSION   The aim of this brief essay has been simply to suggest how the rather fleshless skeleton of the classical conception of the ecclesial relation may be clothed with flesh and animated with blood. The skeleton remains; the classical conception of the vertical relationship of authority and freedom. But it needs to assume a more Christian and therefore more human form by standing forth in the living flesh and blood that is the Christian community. More abstractly, the vertical relationship of command-obedience needs to be completed by the horizontal relationship of dialogue between authority and the free Christian community. The two relationships do not cancel, but reciprocally support, each other.

This more adequate understanding of the ecclesial relationship does not indeed dissolve the inevitable tension between freedom and authority. But by situating this perennial polarity within the living context of community, it can serve to make the tension healthy and creative, releasing the energies radiant from both poles for their one common task, which is to build the beloved community.

Authority and Freedom

in the Christian Community,

Expressed in the Structures

of the Institution

Eugene Fontinell

Apology By Way of a Preface[1]

It was with no little reluctance that I agreed to submit this paper. The reasons for my reluctance were: 1) We Roman Catholics have just about talked and written the authority-freedom question to death; 2) I find it hard to imagine that I could say anything to the participants of the Symposium which they have not already heard or read *ad nauseam*. Nevertheless, I agreed to attempt a paper for a number of reasons among which the following might be noted:

---

1. I decided against changing the form in which this paper was originally written despite the obvious fact that it was intended to be read *and* discussed rather than merely read. The reason quite simply is that the somewhat choppy and staccato form employed enabled me to state my views with a sharpness and directness which would be hard to retain in a more smooth-flowing essay. I have not even tried to purge the paper of a few traces of humor. After all, if one is going to call for such a far-reaching and radical reconstruction of Catholicism as I do, the least one can do is smile while doing it. I hope, however, that this will not be misunderstood as a frivolous, "top-of-the-head" iconoclasm. Hence, I have in several places referred to articles in which I spell-out in a bit more detail the rationale behind the conclusions which I state here with such brutal simplicity.

Mr. Eugene Fontinell is the Chairman of the Department of Philosophy, Queen's College, City University of New York, and Chairman of the Institute For Freedom in The Church. His Ph.D. in Philosophy was awarded by Fordham University. Mr. Fontinell is an associate editor of CROSS CURRENTS, *and he has written articles on the philosophy of religion.*

1) Because I firmly believe in the value and necessity of institutional reform and I think that it is of no little significance that concrete leadership is being given by the representatives of the most scorned institution within the Church (I refer to Canon Law as an institution not necessarily to the Canon Law Society).

2) Because I believe that the most crying need within the Church at the moment is *communication*—in particular with institutional representatives. To be more specific, communication between the hierarchy and the *others,* whether those others are called lay people, clergy or religious. (The hierarchy here would include not only the bishops but those whose position or function in the Church lead them to see themselves as extensions or special representatives of the bishops. Hence, the hierarchy might conceivably include some individuals who appear to be laymen.)

3) Because the Chairman of the Symposium made quite clear to me that "the paper is not intended to be a detailed and scholarly research piece but simply a position statement, a frame of reference, a series of observations which you feel to be most pertinent."

I fully intend to take advantage of this open invitation and hence will make no attempt to present anything approaching a well-rounded paper on my topic. Keeping in mind that the paper is for the purposes of discussion, I will not be concerned with smooth transitions or inner unity. Instead, I will endeavor to indicate the nature of my perspective and the direction in which I think that it would and should lead us. Since we are "dialoguing" and not debating, I do not feel compelled to offer "proof" for my all too general assertions. Needless to say, I am not asking anyone to accept what I say without question. I merely ask that it not be rejected out-of-hand simply because it does not immediately appear to be reconcilable with the usual interpretation of Roman Catholicism.

In the interest of space, allow me to make a blanket apology for the following: for being too personal, for being too general, for stating commonplaces as if they were radically new insights, for failing to qualify adequately my statements, for raising questions which I cannot answer and, what is even worse, for answering questions which no one has raised.

160

I / Controlling Assumptions [2]

1) Everyone possesses what might variously be called a fundamental perspective, a set of basic assumptions, a world-view or a metaphysics. Whether explicit or implicit, whether articulated or unarticulated, this metaphysics colors, influences and in great part forms our thought and action.

2) Ultimately, every metaphysic involves an act of faith in that it is an irreducible affirmation, which is unprovable.

3) There is no Roman Catholic or even Christian metaphysics. This is not to say that any and every metaphysics is able to be employed by or reconciled with Christianity. It does say, however, that the issue cannot be settled simply by showing that particular metaphysics is in conflict with that classical metaphysics employed so long and so well by the Church.

4) The metaphysics which I believe to have the most possibility for the needed reconstruction of Christianity is characterized by process and relations rather than permanence and substances. Such a metaphysics excludes any dualism which divides reality into the substantially unchanging and the accidentally changing.

5) There are no absolutes, whether values, essences or laws, which have their reality and identity independent of history and process. I would contend that this position does not necessarily result in a destructive relativism. A relativism or relationalism it most assuredly is but one which is able to avoid a narrowing individualism and to account for continuity and a kind of permanence.

6) The ultimate criterion of values, laws or institutions is the quality of life which emerges from them. Hence some form of the pragmatic method must be employed which enables us to be sensitive to and act upon the cumulative experience of persons and the community.

---

2. For a more extended treatment of my position on the points raised in this section see, "Reflections on Faith and Metaphysics," *Cross Currents* (Winter, 1966), pp. 15-40; and "Religious Truth In A Relational and Processive World," *Cross Currents* (Summer, 1967), pp. 284-315.

II / Some Observations

1) A shift in one's basic perspective or fundamental assumptions transforms everything else. Thus the apparently same statement made by individuals whose underlying assumptions are radically different will have strikingly different implications. For example, Roman Catholic "A" and Roman Catholic "B" both agree that the Church changes or develops. "A," however, assumes that reality is substantially or essentially immutable and that important and evident as change is, it can only belong to the accidental features of reality. "B," on the other hand, assumes that change or process is characteristic of all reality and that while substance and essence may be functionally useful categories, they cannot be used to signify reality or realities which escape change.

The influence which these assumptions have upon institutional reform is obvious. From the point of view of "A," reform will mean the attempt to discover the essential and unchanging institutions of the Church and then to accidentally modify them in such a way that they will be more faithful to what they substantially or essentially always have been and always will be. From the point of view of "B," reform will mean attempting to *create* institutions (as the Church in its early life created them) which will better serve the Church's ever-developing life.

(Though my position is obviously that of "B," I in no way wish to deny that the other position is both respectable and formidable. Nor do I wish to suggest that the position which I am affirming is without profound difficulties. Further, while insisting that the radical and conflicting difference of these assumptions will pervade all discussion and action, I am not suggesting that such a difference rules out joint discussion and cooperative action. I believe in dialogue between Roman Catholics as well as between Roman Catholics and non-Catholics.)

2) God the message-sender or God the institution-founder or God the law-giver, all are dead. These are ways in which the community at an earlier time conceived and conceptualized its experience with God and while they were important and helpful for a time they are now obstacles to the Church's continuing realization of itself. I would quickly add that God as the *encompassing* in whose presence we struggle to act responsibly and to realize our tasks may be very much alive. God as the "nameless one" who encounters man in history and calls him to join and share in the great undertaking of redemptive creation may still evoke a life of faith on the part of men.

162

3) The mission of the Church is to create and not imitate. In its most formative moments the Church was creative. Whatever criticisms might be advanced against the medieval church there is no denying that it was where the action was. While the Church can no longer deceive itself into thinking that it is the exclusive creative principle in man's redemptive development, it must once again become *a* creative principle.

4) The notions of "divine institutions" and "divine laws" as they are generally understood within the Church are obstacles to its development. Such an attitude leads us to expend our energies in attempting to discover these institutions and in the process to be continually shoring-up institutions which have had their day. If, on the other hand, laws and institutions are creations of the human community (perhaps in response to a Divine Call) for which we are responsible before God, then perhaps our energies would be employed in fashioning institutions and laws which further the development of human life. It is time for us to cease blaming God for what we produce. This is not to take a negative view toward human productions but rather to avoid wrapping these productions in a Divine aura and thereby excuse ourselves from the continuing task of producing better and more adequate institutions.

5) Though I am using the Roman Catholic Church as my primary focus, I am not implying that the problems of institutional reform and the relationship between authority and freedom are exclusively Roman Catholic—nor even Christian or religious in the restricted sense of those terms. The Roman Catholic Church is, in a telescoped fashion, undergoing changes that have been taking place in the western world for over 400 years. The collapse of stable institutions, of absolute values, of world order and the accompanying sense of loss is characteristic of 20th century man. It is only recently however, that it is being suggested that Roman Catholics can share this uncertainty, anguish and alienation. Even more, it is being suggested that one can be an authentic Christian *only* if one shares this anguish. Hence Christianity, from this perspective, is no longer defended as an answer to or a release from the human condition. We may believe, however, that it is a way of living this condition which lends meaning, dimension and direction to it.

6) Can an institution reform itself from the top down? No! Can an institution reform itself in such a way that it avoids the destruction which has characterized most revolutions? Doubtful, but worth a try! However, those who affirm this as a possibility are in self-deception

if they think that this can be done with no pain and by basically continuing "business as usual" within the old store, to which has been added some new window-dressing. This I believe to be the attitude of the Pope and most of the Bishops. "We must not move too fast" becomes an excuse for not daring to be adequate to the task. After all, this is a meaningless phrase for it is equally true to say that "we must not move too slow." The difficulty, of course, is that *a priori* we cannot be certain as to what is "too fast" or "too slow." The evidence at this moment in history would seems to suggest that the Church has been going slow to the point of death.

(One must always guard against neurotically harping on the shortcomings of the Church, but unless there is an awareness of the enormity of the disaffection, unless there is a willingness to recognize that the stagnation which threatens the life of the Church is not restricted to some minor or so-called accidental features of Church life and doctrine, then the effort equal to the task simply will not be forthcoming.)

7) In a sense, the present situation, in which the Roman Catholic leaders think that they are in favor of change while refusing to face up to the implications of real fundamental change, is more frustrating than the pre-Vatican II attitude. For the most part the documents, as such, of Vatican II do not manifest any deep awareness of the profoundly disturbing implications of a developmental man and world. It is not too unfair to say that they represent a long overdue effort of the Church to "catch-up" with the world (it has been suggested that they stand as model statements of enlightened 18th century thought). My impression, however, is that most Bishops view them as revolutionary in themselves and feel that the faithful should be content to study them and put their principles into practice. The real significance of the Council is not so much in the documents themselves, which few Catholics have read closely if at all, as in the collapse of a number of Catholic self-images. A few examples of self-images which have been destroyed by recent events are: all Catholics are in full agreement on the meaning of essential doctrines; Bishops in particular are in agreement (hence the sociological shock of their public disagreement); the Church has, if not all the answers, at least all the necessary answers; a faithful Catholic cannot even entertain the possibility of basic change in the liturgy, or the doctrine on contraception or clerical celibacy.

It is Vatican II as an *event*, therefore, which is significant and I believe radically significant. Actually, the Bishops have wrought better (or worse depending on one's perspective) than they knew or even dreamed. There is a thrust and dynamism bound up with certain words and actions which cannot be completely checked and which is already manifest in the deep unrest which characterizes the Roman Catholic community. Having called for free and responsible thought and action the Bishops are going to have to learn to live with what results without panicking. Perhaps without intending it, the Bishops have loosed a force which I believe to be positive and creative but which also has its threatening dimensions. (It is a bit unsettling to sit in a living room and hear people who but a few short years ago were vehemently expressing the most hide-bound of Roman Catholic positions now giving vent to views that make one's own "radicalism" almost pale by comparison.)

Despite the dangers and difficulties, I am persuaded that there is no turning back and that if we are to retain and develop some of the most dynamic forces and personalities in the Church, we will have to make radical changes and in a relatively short time. It is hard to convey to the leaders of the Church that heresy, materialism, atheism, secularism and the like are no longer the crucial concerns of what I believe to be the most significant element within the Church.

8) So rapid is the change in attitude that even concern for the reform of institutions stamps one as almost irremediably old-fashioned. Proceeding from the valid awareness that the Church is not reducible to its institutional forms, many are fully convinced that the best approach is to let these forms fall of their own weight and in the meantime to get on with the pressing problems of mankind. Such persons in no way feel that they are surrendering their Christianity or even that they are outside the Church. I think that for many people it is quite proper that they pursue this course and not hang themselves up on matters which too quickly become parochial. At the same time I am not persuaded that this is *the* way for all concerned Catholics or Christians. I think that institutional reform remains one of the pressing needs not only of Catholics but of all men. After all, one of the continuing central problems of mankind is how to develop a society which does not smother the person in an external authority and order nor fragment him into an individualistic and anarchical chaos. Desperate as the situation is in the larger community, I believe that for some time now the civic community has been in advance of the Church. As a minimum, therefore, the Church must incorporate the best procedures, values and attitudes which have contributed so much to the development of man. But this is by no means enough. The Church should be a frontier patrol, not a rear-guard camp.

There is no question of placing the Church in competition with the political community. On the contrary it should recognize that it has advantages and possibilities not normally available to the political community. It should stand as a symbol of the ever present need and effort of men to overcome their antagonisms and divisions. But it must not be an empty symbol continually justifying the real corruption which characterizes it by referring to an *ideal* Church which is beyond criticism. Only as it incarnates its vision and values can the Church make any claim upon the allegiance of mankind. It should not fear making mistakes or taking dead-end turns. It has no blueprint from God whereby it can walk through the battlefield of life untouched and unscarred. It should only fear "copping-out" by refusing to have the daring to pursue its mission—which mission cannot be separated from the risk-laden creative activity which we *believe* is the response to the Divine call.

9) Ironic Note: Least free members of the Church are the Pope and Bishops. We tend to forget that just as the faithful have a right and obligation to share in the authority of the Church, so the Pope and Bishops have a right and obligation to share in its freedom. Perhaps the greatest and most pressing task we have is to free the Pope and the Bishops, and this can be done only by a radical change in the institutions of the papacy and the episcopacy. This cannot be too much stressed. The problem is not that the Pope and Bishops are villains. Some undoubtedly are, but this is really secondary. The problem is that they are the captives of institutions which consume and corrupt the best of them. As long as we delude ourselves into thinking that it is just a matter of getting good Bishops we will never really break the bind which threatens the life of the Church.

Hypothesis: Good institutions can do more to reform weak individuals than strong individuals can to reform bad institutions.

Non sequitur conclusion: The height of folly would be to chain the great vision and mission of the Church to the institution of the Papacy or even the Episcopacy. I do not rule out that these institutions may in some form be defensible but if they are, then this must be shown in terms of the good of the community. Failing that, we cannot retreat into a mystique which places itself beyond reflection, reasonable criticism and the lessons of experience.

10) Whatever theoretical arguments might be advanced in favor of the "in me see Christ" mentality, I think that the evidence of his-

torical experience indicates that it is more harmful than good—harmful to the community as a whole and in particular to those who are burdened with "being Christ" and fearing that anything they say or do will be a reflection upon God.

We have spent too much time and energy "protecting" God (it might not be irreverent to suggest that God is quite capable of taking care of Himself). Further, it has become increasingly clear that for the most part it has been our own egos (collective as well as individual) or creations which we have been so feverishly protecting.

It is nonsensical to continue to maintain that one loses respect for someone who makes and admits he makes mistakes. Undoubtedly there are some people who cannot tolerate the idea that their leaders are human and hence fallible, but there is strong psychological evidence that such an absolutistic mentality or authoritarian personality is unhealthy to say the least. Ironically, no Pope has publicly admitted his shortcomings more than John XXIII and none has been more respected in modern times.

A much greater evil emerges from the failure of those in authority to concede their humanity, namely the evil of *cynicism*. (It should be noted that we find this in politics, the family, and the classroom as well as in the Church.) Cynicism might be described as the "death of the spirit" in that it kills man's faith, hope and love—all of which are necessary for man to continue his struggle. Very simply cynicism is the attitude expressed in the phrase "you can't fight city-hall." Among Catholics there would seem to be what might be called "hard cynicism" and "soft cynicism." "Hard" cynicism is manifest in a "to hell with them" attitude and leads to either an explicit rejection of the Church or a nominal affiliation. "Soft" cynicism is found extensively among those employed directly by Church institutions—in Catholic colleges, hospitals, chancery offices and the like, as well as among curates and members of religious orders. Such people are aware that they are operating in a destructive situation but refuse to act openly against it whether through lack of courage, laziness or that pseudo-piety which cloaks itself in the "unfathomable will of God" and the "mysterious workings of the Holy Spirit."

Irony: Those who vehemently criticize and revolt against the institutions of the Church are at least concerned enough with it to attempt to do something about what they believe to be wrong with it. This is not to say that every criticism is just and every revolt reasonable but as a minimum the leaders ought to establish contact with these energies in the hope of enabling them to become constructive. Too often the Church leaders insist on seeing criticism and revolt as a *cause* of disharmony rather than as an *expression* of a deep disharmony which already exists.

11) We must be willing to bring our personal perspectives to the community for analysis, criticism, refinement and development. But we must *all* be willing to do this, including the Pope and the Bishops. If the Bishops or even the Pope insist that they have some "magic pipeline" to the Holy Spirit and that their position is *the* Catholic position then it is foolish to talk about the need for full communal dialogue or search. I regret the harshness of my language but I firmly believe that any isolated or special charism doctrine must be submitted to the closest scrutiny. If we take seriously the Church as mystery, then we must be willing to submit even our most cherished doctrines to reflection, critical analysis, change and possibly surrender. This does not mean that we will necessarily and always surrender them. If what we believe is really worth believing and striving to realize and incarnate, then it will survive the severest criticism. Sometimes I think that there is no greater sign of the weakness and even lack of faith than the effort to place what one believes in some privileged sanctuary.

12) Popeolatry and infallibileolatry (*mea culpa*) remain serious blocks to creative thinking and acting on the part of Roman Catholics. I am willing to concede that these may be crude expressions of a profoundly significant aspect of the life of the Church, namely, the awareness of itself as the living symbol of God's promise to stick by man through thick and through thin. But to interpret this as if God were giving special protection to some ghetto community over against the rest of mankind is surely small-minded and unworthy of the magnificence of the Divine promise.

13) We must avoid any "transition mentality" which might be advanced as an explanation for the present situation of Roman Catholicism. We must not imagine that we have somehow slipped-off the solid rock of faith but that once we have made the changes called for by Vatican II, we will once again be ensconced within an impenetrable haven, safe and secure from the sea which rages around us. (I would suggest that the metaphor of the Church as a "rock" has long since outlived its usefulness. Much more apt is the "organism" metaphor in which the Church is continually evolving in concept with the ongoing development of reality at large.)

168

On the assumption of reality as a "flow" or as process we can never again have the luxury and security of supposedly unchanging truth, Church, laws or institutions. Hence the great need for "programmed change" since we obviously cannot live with pure flux or linear chaos. This is the ultimate reason why man has brought forth his institutions and why they have an almost inevitable tendency to freeze and eventually breed their own destruction.

14) *Note*: I do not deny that for just about every assertion I have made there are reasonable and formidable alternatives probably much better grounded in Christian tradition. Still I must assert that the world-view which permeates those traditional expressions has collapsed for me and apparently is collapsing for many other Catholics and Christians. *Task*: To reconstruct Christianity in terms of a radically processive world-view. Can this be done? Of course neither I nor anyone else can know the answer with any degree of certainty. We can, however, *believe* in its possibility, which means that we must be willing to literally "stake our lives" on bringing it to realization while all the time we are aware that we might be heading over a precipice. This risk dimension, in my opinion, is by no means restricted to those who believe in the radical reconstruction of Christianity—it is the mark of any and every significant faith.

III / Institutions and Reforms [3]

1) Institutions are the means to the realization of values and vision but we must guard against using the necessity of institutions as a justification for continuing obsolete and destructive ones. Irony: "institutional types" are the great enemies of institutions because by transforming these institutions into "idols" they prevent them from making the contribution which they are intended to make and this eventually breeds an excessive anti-institutional mentality.

Hence, it is a grave error to identify institutions with the values or the vision which they are intended to serve and help realize. It is no exaggeration to say that this is idolatry.

2) The fundamental challenge is not to transform this or that particular institution in the Church, though we should certainly

---

3. My position on institutions is developed a bit more fully in, "In Defense of Institutions," *America* (March 4, 1967), pp. 314-316.

do this as much as is possible. In the long run, however, the crucial question is whether it is possible to institutionalize the principle of self-correction. This principle, of course, is one of the great humanizing insights developed by the institution of modern science. While to some extent this principle has been built into the Anglo-Saxon political community, I do not believe that we have even begun consciously to incorporate it into our religious communities. It would seem that a community which sees itself as "the pilgrim church" would be most apt for the utilization of this principle. A self-correcting community, however, would have to give its primary allegiance to the manifest quality of community life and not to allegedly first principles or unchanging truths.

3) Closely allied to and involved in the principle of self-correction is that of experimentation. Again, I would suggest that this is no narrow technical principle peculiar to science but is humanistic in the sense of being bound up with all aspects of human life. Needless to say, the mode of experimentation will vary with the dimension of reality with which it is concerned. In the broadest sense, however, it means the willingness to strike out in some direction (whether in thought or action) with no certainty of the outcome and at the same time being willing to change direction when experience indicates a dead-end or destructive turn.

4) I would suggest that any Constitution for the Church that does not find a way of building in self-correction and experimentation will hardly survive its writing.

IV / Specifically on Authority and Freedom

1) Neither authority nor freedom are able to be defined once and for all. I would suggest that it is more profitable to view them as functional relationships continually interacting and shifting. Hence, there is no possibility of achieving a mechanical and permanent balance. If we were to think of authority as the principle of order and freedom as the principle of creativity, then we would be stimulated to create fruitful forms of interaction.

2) In recent years Roman Catholics have been saturated with truly brilliant statements about freedom. It is not a reflection on either the necessity nor the quality of these statements to point out that the pressing need is not more such theories but the formation of creative

structures and institutions which will enable the vision and insight involved in such theories to be lived. The only significant freedom is lived freedom and there is no lived freedom apart from institutions which bring it forth.

3) Henceforth, the only suitable structures will be those which presuppose the developmental nature of man, the world and the Church. Further, fruitful interaction rather than destructive conflict will be possible between the person and the community only when we have come to a fuller realization of their inseparability and interdependence. Whatever our problems are, we cannot even begin to resolve them as long as explicitly or implicitly we continue to think of an individual as an atomistic entity having its essence and nature in itself and in isolation from others and to think of a community as an undifferentiated mass absorbing and annihilating the uniqueness and personality of its members. When, however, we recognize that the human person is the individualized focus or expression of the community, that paradoxically we can achieve greater individuality only by greater participation in community, then at least we are aware that any either-or resolution is unacceptable.

In addition, the perspective of both the individual and the community will be transformed. The individual person becomes obligated to attempt to determine whether or not his actions respect his varied relationships and are thereby in keeping with the deepest ideals of his community or communities by which he is continually being formed. On the other hand, the community must ever be on guard against betraying itself in the direction of a choking uniformity through a failure to recognize its most insightful and farseeing representatives.

The role of the prophet would seem to illustrate this. The prophet, assuming that he is not a false prophet, is not an egotistical rugged individualist who places himself in neurotic opposition to the community. Rather, he is the one who at a particular moment in the life of the community is the best expression of the community inasmuch as he illumines the community's self-betrayal and urges it to be faithful to the vision and ideals which give to it its identity.[4]

---

4. The material in the preceding few paragraphs is excerpted from a lecture, "Towards An Ethics of Relationships," originally given at the Institute for Religious and Social Studies, Jewish Theological Seminary of America. It will appear in a volume entitled, *Ethics, Theology and Change*, edited by John J. McDermott.

4) I believe that we Roman Catholics have too often posed the problem in terms of either authority or no authority, while I think that since the time of Rousseau and Kant the crucial question has been *external* versus *internal* authority. Modern man has quite properly, in my opinion, rejected all authority which is imposed from without, an authority in which the members of the community have no effective share or participation. I know that this touches a raw nerve but I would contend that the "divine right" of popes and bishops is no more acceptable than the "divine right" of kings. The decisive factor here is not the belief that authority is in some way from God but whether it is directly from God to the Pope and the Bishops. On the direct source view, there is no appeal from the decisions of authority. This introduces an element of magic and mystique that I believe has shown itself to be destructive rather than liberating.

5) The Church stands in desperate need of democratization. Just as experimentation is not restricted to science, democratization cannot be restricted to politics. It is a great mistake to reduce democracy to a particular political form or set of voting procedures. The indispensable humanistic element in democracy can be expressed in one word—*participation*. While man is far from having realized and incarnated the insight embodied in democracy, at least he has come to recognize that those communities which tend toward maximizing the participation of their members have more liberating results and possibilities than those which exclude their members from responsible roles in the *fundamental* formative life of the community. I fully agree that it is much easier to call for participation of the members of the community than to show how this can be achieved. Nevertheless I would submit that we will not even begin to move in this direction unless we really believe that this should be our goal.

6) It is now evident that any restructuring of the Church cannot be done solely by the Bishops nor by the Bishops aided by the theologians. Ways must be found to bring the full weight of cumulative human (not merely Catholic or Christian) experience to this enormous undertaking. I have not nor cannot supply the detailed *how* of this endeavor but I have tried to suggest that the "mind-set" which undergirds this effort will have tremendous influence on just what results.

The Polity and Politics

of Church Unity

Keith Bridston

Church unity presents us with both a juridical problem and a political problem. The juridical problem is better known and understood. The issue is clear. The law and polity of the churches are different. These differences have, at least in the past, divided the Christian community. There are, of course, superficial reasons for this. Juridical forms and practices represent long-standing habits and styles of community life. They embody the ethos of a group. They incarnate a way of existence. What is familiar and customary for one church in its juridical manners is strange and exotic to another. For simple psychological reasons, just as in regard to liturgical behaviour, these differences present barriers to mutual understanding and fellowship.

But at a deeper level, these varying juridical forms also manifest profound ecclesiological divergences between the churches. As Lukas Vischer, Director of the Faith and Order Commission of the World Council of Churches, has written: "The question about the proper 'juridical' form of the Church is an eminently ecumenical problem. When divided churches

Reverend Keith R. Bridston is a professor of Theology at Pacific Lutheran Theological Seminary, a member school of the Graduate Theological Union at Berkeley. A specialist in matters of church order, Professor Bridston worked for several years in the Faith and Order division of the World Council of Churches in Geneva.

meet, they quickly ascertain that their order and external form constitute at least as great a hindrance to their entry into full fellowship as do their faith and doctrine. . . . The question about the proper juridical form of the Church is not an ecumenical problem only because the churches which meet in the ecumenical movement exhibit different structures. . . . The differences which divide the churches in the area of order have deep roots. . . . The differences have their basis in divergent ecclesiologies; therefore they can be overcome when the various churches will be able to broaden and deepen their ecclesiological agreement."[1]

To take one example: If we were to compare the Lutheran and the Roman Catholic views of church order we would find, roughly speaking, that in their classical expressions the Catholic position tends to emphasize that the juridical form of the Church is in its essentials not human but based on *ius divinum,* whereas Lutheran confessions tend to stress that the unity of the Church is found in the Gospel and that where it is proclaimed in its purity there is one Church even though there may be differences in polity.[2]

To exaggerate the issue: In the Roman Catholic tradition canon law is honored and exalted; in the Lutheran it is rejected and neglected. The ecclesiological self-understandings that lie behind these contradictory attitudes are evidently in conflict. For generations that remained the situation. Today, however, from both sides there has been a gradual reappraisal of the classical positions. On the Roman Catholic side, there has been a concerted endeavor to distinguish between the unchanging and immutable *ius divinum* and the flexible and relative *ius mere ecclesiasticum.* On the Lutheran side, there has been an equally critical reevaluation of the traditional spiritualizing outlook in regard to church law and a gradual acceptance of the visible structure of the Church as a reflection of the providential care of God for His people.

Even in that less contradictory form, the ecclesiological issue is far from being resolved. Nevertheless, it is a step forward because the two positions are no longer in direct and irreconcilable juxtaposition to one another. One of the ways of reducing the contradictions even more is the exercise of honest philosophical disciplines such as logic and linguistic analysis by both sides, privately and in concert: do we really mean the same thing when we use the term "law"? What is our understanding of "essential"?

---

1. *The Jurist,* Vol. XXVI, No. 4. Oct. 1966, 395ff.
2. *The Encyclopedia of the Lutheran Church,* Vol. 1, 519ff.

The need for intense dialogue on such issues is obvious. Alfred North Whitehead has pointed out in relation to scientific advances that contradictions, if properly maintained in creative polarity, are the beginnings of new insights which transcend the limitations of the former antitheses, both incorporating the basic truths of the former positions and yet going beyond them. One of Whitehead's warnings may be kept in mind as a wise word for ecumenical explorations of this type: contradictions should not be abandoned prematurely because, as he says, there are no "short-cuts" on the road of truth. Sentimentally motivated syntheses are no substitute for the true unity achieved through faithfulness to the truth as each party sees it, slow and painful as that way often is.

Historical disciplines are also useful in the search for an ecumenical rapprochement on church polity. To take another example: Luther is popularly stereotyped as the radical revolutionary, burning the canon law with one hand and shaking his fist against the papacy with the other. But recent Luther studies, both Protestant and Roman Catholic, are a sharp corrective to such caricatures. One of the pioneering Catholic monographs in this field, Franz Xaver Arnold's *Zur Frage Des Naturrechts Bei Martin Luther* (1936), prefigures a flood of later literature which show the general acceptance of Luther of the main assumptions of medieval doctrines of natural law. As Luther writes to the German nobility, in his famous tract of 1520, his opposition to canon law is based on the fact that "the canon law contains so many heretical and unchristian, nay unnatural laws"; ecclesiastical laws as such are, he writes, "good," but "only so long as they are not injurious to Christianity and the laws of God." This is clearly not far removed from the position of Aquinas, for instance, which modern historical scholarship has also reviewed and emphasized the extent to which his idea of natural law frees the Church from the necessity of justifying every order, structure, and legislation as the direct will of God.

As an ecumenical fruit of this type of historical reappraisal of the traditions we find Gustaf Wingren of Lund arguing that the Lutheran insistence on the freedom of the Church to have a variety of polities is a theory of *order* and not of anarchy.[3] Freedom of form *is*, says Wingren, an ecclesiological principle and not a matter of indifference. It is a theology of form, not an ideology of chaos. On the other side, Hans Kung and Karl Rahner, among others, are, without challenging essential Catholic theology of order, arguing that precisely that doctrine allows, and indeed demands,

---

3. *Svensk Teologisk Kvartalskrift,* 1958.

distinctions to be made between the divinely constituted elements of the Church's corporate existence and the historically conditioned and thus relative manifestations of this primal order "exposed to man's freedom, to his whims and to his errors."[4]

Here again, the classical Protestant-Catholic conflict over the question of freedom and form is being seen in a new light, from a new perspective, which transcends the previous, apparently irreconcilable, contradictions. And one might suppose that similar differences in regard to the form and order of the Church between other Christian bodies also be gradually resolved by analogous historical and philosophical enterprises. The fact is that the new ecumenical climate both permits and invites such mutual endeavors and, if the opportunity is grasped, many of the old conflicts over church order may already be a thing of the past by the very act of talking together about them in love and without defensiveness. In so doing, we not only see the other party (and its positions) in a new way, but (perhaps more importantly) ourselves.

In short, the differences of church polity do not appear to be the insuperable hindrances to church unity that they once were. Polities are changing. Moreover, existing differences are being seen not simply as expressions of insurmountable ecclesiological divisions but, in many instances, as legitimate varieties of manifestation of the same fundamental theological convictions. Such differences do not divide the Church, or should not, because through such variety the whole Body is enriched and the whole People is equipped, through the various gifts of the Spirit, to fulfill its apostolic ministry in all times, in all places, for all men and nations. If the churches can together agree on the minimal essentials of church order, this theological consensus can provide the basis for a more catholic understanding of the varieties of polity which are available to the Christian community in structuring its common life for effective witness and service in the modern world. Variety of forms is divisive if it is conceived in a sectarian spirit; but variety of forms understood in a catholic spirit can be seen as a manifestation of the variety of gifts of the Holy Spirit equipping the Body for its service.

There remains, however, another dimension of the problem which might be called political. The Church as an institution has a constitutional structure. This is its polity. But it also has its political life. James

---

4. K. Rahner & J. Ratzinger, *The Episcopate and the Primacy,* 13.

Gustafson of Yale in his study of church institutionalism *Treasure in Earthen Vessels* distinguishes between "church order" and "church politics," the latter being "the process by which decisions are made and actions taken." If it were possible through the dialogical methodology already mentioned to harmonize the now conflicting polities of the separated churches, and this does not seem as unlikely as it once did, as has been said, the question would still remain: What is in fact the relation between the polities and politics of the churches?

It might be assumed that the politics of a particular ecclesiastical institution arise naturally and logically out of its polity. Recent sociological analyses make this thesis less and less tenable. Since 1957 the Faith and Order Commission of the World Council of Churches has undertaken a depth study of institutionalism. It has been posited on the "commonplace," in the words of the former chairman of the study group, Dean Walter Muelder of Boston, "that religion in its organizational aspects is marked by the same human problems as social life in general."[5] A number of case studies, largely drawn from Protestantism, arising out of the work of the study group have been published in the volume *Institutionalism* (edited by Walter Muelder and Nils Ehrenstrom). These cases make it crystal clear that there is often a sharp discrepancy between the formal polities of the churches and their informal politics. The constitutional form of an ecclesiastical body is no sure guide to its political processes. For instance, formal authority may be vested in certain stated officers—bishops, presidents, superintendents, etc.—but the effective political power may rest elsewhere in other hands. In certain Protestant churches, especially in the free church tradition, there is strong antipathy to centralized authority and the formal polity of these bodies is a constitutional embodiment of this conviction. Nevertheless, if their political processes are analyzed, a secondary institutional form emerges. As D. O. Moberg in *The Church as a Social Institution* summarizes the situation: "Powerful boards dominated by executive secretaries play a major part in the government of congregations and denominations. The drive for unity and efficiency tends to overcome anti-bureaucratic theological doctrines."

In other words, the form of polity and the form of politics of a church do not necessarily coincide. Indeed, if American Protestantism provides any indication, coincidence between polity and politics is the exception rather than the rule in the churches. Vatican II revealed an analo-

---

5. *Bulletin*, Vol. VI, No. 1. Division of Studies, ECC.

gous situation in Roman Catholicism. During the course of the Council it became transparent that real political power was being held and exercised by individuals and groups for which there was little or no authorization in terms of classical Catholic polity. The power of the Curia over against that of the Council as such, which created many of the conflicts and tensions of the assembly, is a vivid case in point.

Though such phenomena may seem strange to those who have been accustomed to view the Church through traditional spectacles, it is a "commonplace" to the social scientists. In fact, much of the work of the sociologists and political scientists in the field of organizational and institutional behaviour is spent in analyzing such phenomena and providing a systematic explanation of it. One of the most fascinating papers presented to the Faith and Order institutionalism study group was "The Function and Control of Power in the Church in Relation to the Question of Unity and Disunity" by J. Milton Yinger of Oberlin. While admitting that the church (as any social institution) has its own peculiar characteristics, Yinger makes a persuasive argument for the applicability of the major insights of the social sciences in regard to institutional forms and processes to the life of the churches. The "power dilemma" having to do with the "distribution of power within an organization" is not significantly different in the political existence of the churches than it is in a large-scale business corporation or labor union or political party. They each have their own special ethos, goals, protocol, and traditions which condition the precise form which their politics take but the general political pattern is more or less common. One probably gets a more accurate depiction of this in such fictional works as Power's *Morte d'Urban,* West's *Shoes of the Fisherman,* or, from the Protestant side, Wilson's *Stained Glass Jungle,* than in traditional church histories or text-books in ecclesiology! As Yinger says: "Religious groups often resist the implication that their staffs are concerned with orderly career patterns, with status, with power. Failure to recognize these interests complicates the problem of deflection rather than eliminating it. . . . The main point is that the church cannot escape the dilemmas of power."[6]

One may ask what the relevance of all this is for the unity of the Church? Certain implications seem to be clear. In the first place, the problem of church unity cannot be dealt with solely on the level of formal church polity. The differences of polity, past or present, are not decisive indices of either unity or disunity. Similarity of polity may only

---

6. Ibid.

disguise fundamental differences of political procedure and process. Dissimilarities in polity may equally camouflage fundamental agreement in political theory and practice. Or, to put it another way, a phenomenological assessment of the politics of the divided churches may reveal a more basic and pervasive similarity between the separated bodies than their formal polities would suggest. For example, the political role of a Roman Catholic parish priest and that of a Protestant congregational minister may, and seem to be in fact, far more identical than their respective constitutional positions as defined by polity would argue. The same would appear to be true of a Catholic bishop and a Protestant church president. One of the Protestant observers at Vatican II was quoted in an interview on returning to New York as having said: "They lack a good chairman." Behind all the facade of baroque pageantry, liturgical splendour, and exotic protocol he had perceived a church assembly at work. To that extent he could identify with it and, accurately or not, criticize its political procedures. In terms of polity he was a stranger; politically he was at home.

What this may suggest is that agreement of church politics is more urgent than agreement on polity in preparing the way for unity between the churches. If, for example, it could be seen that the Consultation on Church Union deliberations on the organizational pattern of the projected united church are dealing with the same political issues as those facing the Catholics in pondering the respective roles of the Pope and the college of bishops a certain sense of a communal enterprise in the interests of unity might begin to pervade the whole Christian community. It is not only in the church that common problems weld bonds of fellowship and unity.

In the second place, however, it is essential, in the words of Benedetto Croce, to achieve in the mind of the Church "an elevation of pure politics to an ethical position." As Croce says: "There can be no moral life that is not both economic and political life, just as there can be no soul without a body. And moral man does not put into practice his morality except by acting in a political manner and by accepting the logic of politics." As an illustration Croce refers to the struggles of St. Bernard with King Ruggiero of Sicily, as well as to Protestantism itself which, he observes, was "forced from the very beginning to adopt political methods" learned, he believes, "from its Jesuit adversaries, excellent teachers of such matters in theory and in practice."[7]

---

7. *Politics,* 22.

The idea of politics as a moral discipline does not come easily to churchmen, probably because of persistent traces of docetic other-worldliness and ethical perfectionism in the Western Christian tradition. Notwithstanding, the rejection of politics and a denial of the "dilemma of power" in the churches does away with neither politics nor power. Rather it leads to bad politics and corrupt power, as Bertrand Russell has so vividly chronicled in his searing criticism of ecclesiastical political hypocrisy in his book *Power*. Or as Reinhold Niebuhr puts it: "In one sense the presence or absence of cynicism among the oligarchs is beside the point. The important point is that the ruthless power operates behind a screen of pretended ideal ends, a situation which is both more dangerous and more evil than pure cynical defiance of moral ends. It corresponds to the weakness of the human heart more nearly than absolute cycnicism, for men are less inclined to pure cynicism than to the delusion that they serve some noble purpose in engaging in projects which serve their own end."[8]

Ultimately, the movement for church unity must come to terms with the question of *why* is unity desired and the equally relevant one of *what kind* of unity is appropriate for the Christian Church. A unity which lacks apostolic intention is intolerable. A unity which lacks the quality of holiness is immoral. One thing all churches today have in common: A political life which, possibly because it has been denied and falsified, does not invite close scrutiny. Perhaps one thing which will help to draw the churches together is a common acceptance of the need for reforming their politics. Here again, it is not only in the Church that a common vision and a common task can create strong ties of fellowship and unity. Mutual confession of sins is certainly one of the absolute preconditions for a movement of unity which deserves the name Christian. Martin Marty in reviewing Kaufman's The *Faith of a Heretic,* summarizes his "final indictment" of organized religion: "The churches are preaching against bad faith, dishonesty, poor ethics, immorality—and at the same time, through their self-seeking institutionalism, they are serving to promote bad faith, dishonesty, poor ethics, immorality."[9] Is a united Christendom any better than a divided one on this basis?

As with all politics, church politics can be good or bad. And it may be that the unity of the Church waits upon that time when the politics of the divided churches are good enough to deserve the unitive power of the Spirit.

---

8. *The World Crisis and American Responsibility,* 55-6.
9. *Christian Century,* Nov. 29, 1961.

One final note. Perhaps a deeper appreciation for the political dynamics in the life of the Church will provide a whole new ecclesiological perspective for modern Christianity. The classical focus on polity in respect to church unity betrays a rigid and structural assumption about the essential nature of the Church. Frank Lloyd Wright opened up a whole new era in architecture with his organic principle: Form follows Function.[10] A more functional understanding of ecclesiastical ontology may by-pass many of the traditional barriers to church unity. A deeper awareness of the *functional* essentials of the true Church would provide a new sense of freedom in searching out and developing those forms and polities which would be appropriate to them. Thus, to view the traditional "marks" of the Church—One, Holy, Catholic, Apostolic—as functional rather than structural would turn attention away from the intransigent problems of polity to those of politics, away from static and formal conceptions of the Church to a dynamic and organic one.

This reconceptualization of ecclesiology in more dynamic terms, the revisualization of the Church as process rather than structure, as organism rather than institution, as functional rather than formal, as political rather than juridical, may prepare the way for that transformation and renewal of the Body of Christ in the world which, among other things, may mean a more adequate and vital manifestation of its essential unity.

This "renewing of the mind" of the Church is a *sine qua non* for the realization of church unity. Eric Mascall, the Anglo-Catholic theologian, suggests in one of his books on the ecumenical movement that it is the agreement rather than the disagreement which separate Christians. That is, unexamined common assumptions which all unconsciously accept, but from which contradictory conclusions are drawn, most radically divide the Christian communities. In the most recent issue of *Daedalus,* "Toward the Year 2000," Lawrence Frank pleads the case for a new political theory: "We urgently need a new political theory to replace that which was formulated in the late-eighteenth century and has become cumulatively inadequate and frustrating for the present and an impediment for the future." He argues that existing political theory is derived from a conception of society which had as its model "the celestial machinery of Newton." Today, however, the shape of society and the forces at work within it are too multiform and complex to be understood or to be coped with on the basis of outmoded Newtonian conceptual models. As Frank says: "We have no adequate conception

---

10. *Frank Lloyd Wright: Writings and Buildings,* ed. E. Kaufmann & B. Raeburn

of such a dynamic organization. Traditionally, organization has been conceived of as a hierarchical entity and illustrated by charts with a chain of command from the top to the lower echelons and individuals. Some definitions are offered as static models that are supposed to operate, but there is no clearly stated theory of how they work. Today we are beginning to recognize that organisms and human organizations are persistent configurations of functioning processes closely coupled and entrained and engaged in circular, reciprocal operations involving feedbacks."[11]

In physics, biology, engineering and other social, technological and scientific fields this kind of reconceptualization, with a new cosmological vision, is leading to creative breakthrough identified with such dynamic theories as "open systems," "self-organizing systems," "cybernetics" and others. An analogous ecumenical re-vision of the Church is needed to transcend the barriers to fuller manifestations of unity rooted in anachronistic conceptual models which have informed the various ecclesiologies and presented irreconcilable contradictions and which cannot be resolved as long as the Newtonian, or pre-Newtonian, intellectual models are still commonly assumed. This raising up of new dynamic models of the Church is also required in order that the ecumenical vision of the Church of the future is not beclouded by antique preconceptions of what true Church unity might be. Thus, the classical juridical model gives way to a political one, and the political is qualified by a sociological one, and it, in turn, must be qualified by new models as yet unseen and unknown.

In short, our vision of the Church and its unity must not be constricted by the limitations of the operative conceptual models of the past which impose restraints on either our memory or our imagination of what God can, has done, and will do. For it is not our conceptual inhibitions which will determine the shape of the Church of tomorrow but the free movement of the Spirit, Who "blows where He wills." Whitehead hopefully suggests that man by means of "symbolic transference can achieve miracles of sensitiveness to a distant environment, and to a problematic future" but warns that "those societies which cannot combine reverence to their symbols with freedom of revision, must ultimately decay either from anarchy, or from the slow atrophy of a life stifled by useless shadows."[12]

---

11. *Journal of the American Academy of Arts and Sciences,* Vol. 93, No. 3, Summer, 1967, 809ff.
12. ed. Rollo May, *Symbolism in Religion and Literature,* 249-50.

INDEX